Bass Guitar Exercises

by Patrick Pfeiffer

Foreword by Mark Egan

Bass Guitar Exercises For Dummies®

Published by: John Wiley & Sons, Inc., 111 River Street, Hoboken, NJ 07030-5774, www.wiley.com

Copyright © 2020 by John Wiley & Sons, Inc., Hoboken, New Jersey

Published simultaneously in Canada

For general information on our other products and services, please contact our Customer Care Department within the U.S. at 877-762-2974, outside the U.S. at 317-572-3993, or fax 317-572-4002. For technical support, please visit www.wiley.com/techsupport.

Library of Congress Control Number: 2020931187

ISBN 978-1-119-70011-1 (pbk); ISBN 978-1-119-70016-6 (ebk); ISBN 978-1-119-70081-4 (ebk)

Manufactured in the United States of America

V10017985_031320

Contents at a Glance

Table of Contents

Foreword

Patrick Pfeiffer has done it again, and this time he has created a comprehensive and complete bass studies book for all levels of bassists.

Bass Guitar Exercises For Dummies is a masterwork that presents not only what to practice but how to practice and includes an extensive amount of audio examples that you can play along with.

You'll be able to practice scales, arpeggios, progressions, and grooves, all of which are the building blocks of a great bassist.

This book shows you how to incorporate these techniques and exercises into your own playing, and as a result, you'll make better music.

Bass Guitar Exercises For Dummies is an invaluable resource for all bassists and should be in every bassist's library regardless of their level of ability. I wish I had this book 40 years ago!

Thank you, Patrick, for the fine work.

—Mark Egan

Introduction

L ay down the groove with tight, focused notes and an irresistible feel. Flawlessly navigate the turbulent sea of rhythm and harmony. Ride the deep, articulate, sonorous sound waves of your bass guitar — and do it all with confidence, skill, grace, and joy.

What if a book comes along that makes you a better bass player — no matter your present level — and streamlines your practice routine with efficient and effective exercises that cover all musical aspects of bass playing, including a multitude of techniques in all styles of music?

This is that book. *Bass Guitar Exercises For Dummies* bridges knowing and doing, or, in the case of musicians, theory and playing. Sure, it's important to memorize certain rules, like which scales to use with which chords, but it won't do you any good unless you have the scales firmly embedded in your *muscle memory*, with your hands trained to reach automatically for the proper move.

It's also important to develop muscle memory to play arpeggios, rhythms, grooves, and melodies, and to establish the wherewithal to apply them to different styles. You find exercises in this book to help you smooth your shifts, your string crossings, your attack, and your dynamics — exercises that don't sound like exercises at all because they're written as musical pieces. After all, you want to play *music*.

About This Book

The exercises in *Bass Guitar Exercises For Dummies* go far beyond the conventional practicing of scales, arpeggios, and other etudes. These exercises are *bass*-specific. Playing scales straight up and down may be great for other instruments, but for bass players it doesn't suffice. As a bassist you're also responsible for rhythm and groove; thus, the scales in *Bass Guitar Exercises For Dummies* resolve *harmonically* as well as *rhythmically*. In fact, many of the scale exercises in this book segue straight into grooves that you can use in real songs.

All the exercises are tried and true, truly the best stuff on earth. You can improve your playing literally within days just by doing the exercises. Of course, I don't expect you to play all 227 or so etudes in one day! I group the exercises so that several address each issue, but in slightly different ways. For example, you get to work all four fingers of your fretting hand whether you're practicing permutations or shifting.

Some exercises are short — only a measure or two — and some are quite lengthy, sometimes two pages. I encourage you to transpose each exercise into all keys, even if the exercise is presented in only one. The bass is symmetrical; therefore, your fingering doesn't change, which makes transposing the music an easy task.

At the end of this book you find a list of techniques, including the order in which to practice them. This is definitely not a book you need to read from front to back, in chronological order. In fact, after you read this introduction, I recommend that you skip to the last chapter to see why it's worth practicing the exercises in *Bass Guitar Exercises For Dummies*. There you find examples of exercises applied to famous bass-heavy music, and I assure you, you'll recognize at least some of these songs.

I don't delve into theory very deeply. If you want to know more about a certain scale, groove, or musical style, you may want to look into *Bass Guitar For Dummies*, 2nd Edition (also written by yours truly and published by Wiley). Remember, *Bass Guitar Exercises For Dummies* is an *exercise* book. You get down and dirty and physical. You can listen to each exercise on the accompanying website at www.dummies.com/go/bassguitarexercisesfd (they sound quite cool) as you look at the notation, the tablature, and in some cases the grid. Many of the fingerings and shifts (if applicable) are also indicated. Dive right in — I've got your back.

Conventions Used in This Book

I use a few *For Dummies* conventions in *Bass Guitar Exercises For Dummies* for consistency and to make it easy to follow. To start with, when I refer to the *right hand* I mean your striking hand, and when I refer to the *left hand* I mean your fretting hand. My apologies to southpaws everywhere. Left-handers should translate *right hand* as *left hand* and vice versa (Paul McCartney, are you reading this?).

The fingering numbers are as follows: 1 for the index finger, 2 for the middle finger, 3 for the ring finger, and 4 for the pinkie. The fingering is indicated *above* the notes of the music notation. If you have to move your fretting hand out of position, I indicate this with the word *shift* between the fingering numbers.

Higher and *lower* refer to the pitch, not the physical move. You move from high to low by moving your fretting hand on the neck *away* from the body of the bass and toward the tuning heads. For the striking hand, going from high to low means going from a thin string to a thicker string. It's all about the pitch (did someone yell "strike"?).

In the exercises, the music is printed with the standard music notation on top and the tablature below. If chords are present (for the songs), they're indicated between the notation and the tab. Sometimes you also find a grid nearby to help you visualize the pattern for your fretting hand.

What You're Not to Read

If you'd like to know *why* you're doing what you're doing in an exercise, then by all means read the accompanying text. If you're familiar with a concept, go straight to the notation. I keep the text to a minimum (even though it's a great outlet for my strange sense of humor). I guess you can say it's on a "need-to-know basses."

Foolish Assumptions

I assume you play bass and are somewhat familiar with the concept of scales and chords. You don't have to be an expert yet — this book is supposed to help you become that — but if you need help with the bass-ics, like tuning your bass or buying one, check out *Bass Guitar For Dummies*, 2nd Edition, which is also a great reference source, in case you have any questions about theory. I also assume you're ready to try some fun new material that'll help you fine-tune your bass-playing skills and make you an all-around better, more fluid bass player.

I don't assume you like every style of music that's represented in this book, but I do assume that your favorite is among them. The exercises are aimed at the physical aspect of bass playing, so you can gain the proficiency necessary to play in any style.

How This Book Is Organized

I organize the bulk of the book into four distinct aspects of bass playing: scales (modes), arpeggios (chords), rhythm, and groove genres. Most important, this book shows you how to combine all these aspects into your own playing and to use them to make music.

Part 1: Preparing to Practice

This part is all about getting ready to make the most of your precious practice time, from stretching to posture. You also find a little refresher course on the use of bass notation and tablature, as well as exercises to get the juices in your hands flowing for the workout to come.

Part 2: Scales (Modes) and Chords

Part 2 revels in the exciting world of scales and chords — from playing scales straight up and down to combining them with chord arpeggios and even with grooves. You can find some real ear candy in this part.

Part 3: Rhythm and the Groove

This part lays out all the different elements of a bass groove: the groove skeleton, groove apex, and groove tail. I address each element separately and include musical exercises using real grooves. You also find the so-called *master-maker* etudes here — serious exercises that combine triplets with eighth and sixteenth notes.

Part 4: Turning Exercises into Music

In this part you get to turn the exercises into real-life bass grooves. This part is all about using the right rhythm for the right style — from country to metal, from funk to reggae. You can accumulate a good basic repertoire of genre-specific grooves so that you sound like an expert at your next session.

Part 5: The Part of Tens

This wouldn't be a *For Dummies* book without the Part of Tens. This part gives you the ten essential elements of a complete practice session (along with your very own practice sheet), and you get to see how the exercises in this book are applied in real (and famous) songs. I did tell you that the goal of this book is to get you ready for the big leagues, right?

Part 6: Appendixes

Appendix A gives an overview of the audio tracks you'll find on the website at www.dummies.com/go/bassguitarexercisesfd. Appendix B offers some information for those of you who play extended-range basses, and it gives you a handy worksheet that you can use to keep track of your practices.

The Website

The audio tracks that come with *Bass Guitar Exercises For Dummies* are tracks of me, your author, playing many of the exercises that appear in the book, including some pure performance pieces. Listen to the tracks for examples of how certain exercises should sound. Don't forget that there's room for improvising!

Icons Used in This Book

I don't use many of the typical Dummies icons in this book, but when I do, it's best to pay attention.

TIP

This icon points out expert advice to help you become a better bass player.

REMEMBER

Certain techniques are worth remembering. You may use this information again and again (within and without this book).

TECHNICAL STUFF

This icon alerts you to technical information that you may have missed or forgotten since you first started practicing bass guitar playing.

Where to Go from Here

Go straight to the last chapter (Chapter 15), where you can discover how these exercises can be applied to great music. That should give you an incentive to work through some of the other chapters. If I were you, I'd also check out Chapter 14 to explore the different elements of a great practice session.

Other than that, just dip into each chapter to your heart's content. You certainly don't have to read (or play) through this book in a linear progression. If you're working on getting comfortable with scales, go to Chapter 3. If you want to practice your arpeggios as music, check out Chapter 6. If you can't wait to get your hands on some authentic grooves, jump to Chapter 11. And if you're simply in a rough-and-tough workout mood and want to build up some strength and coordination in your fingers, get it on with Chapter 2.

Whatever you're looking for in a practice routine, I've got you covered. I truly hope that this book enhances your life as a bass player and that you find countless hours of playing pleasure because of it. And when that big gig comes your way, please tell me all about it at my Web site: www.sourkrautmusic.com.

1
Preparing to Practice

Before you start treating practicing as a chore, check out this part to discover how to make it fun, and above all, rewarding. You may never want to leave home again without having had a thorough practice session. You also get a review of some bass-ic fundamentals and a great selection of preparatory stretches and exercises that will have you blazing up and down the fingerboard in no time.

Chapter **1**

Reviewing Practice Fundamentals

know you're just as eager to get started as I am to get you going, but before letting you off the leash, I'd like to make sure you get the most out of your practice time — in terms of skill as well as enjoyment.

In this chapter you find tips on how to structure (and *un*-structure) your bass guitar practice sessions. Some material you're probably familiar with, and other material may be brand-new, but all is very useful to your bass-ic well-being.

How to Approach Practicing Your Bass

Imagine it's the beginning of a perfect day. You're well rested and eager to play, and the only thing on your agenda is to practice bass. Alas, a perfect day indeed. You get comfortable in your bass space, tune your bass guitar, and then . . . and then you wonder how you should be spending your precious practice time.

A primary reason for writing this book is to give you an arsenal of really useful exercises that are fun to play, sound musical, and above all make you a better bass player, so you never again have to wonder what to practice on one of those perfect days when your bass guitar is calling you.

Dividing your practice time

Organizing the time wisely in your practice sessions is one of the most crucial steps you can take to ensure a consistent, effective, and efficient practice routine. First, you need to choose how much time to allot yourself on any given day, and also how much time you can dedicate on a regular basis (it takes more than one session to create a master). Instead of spending the entire practice session slogging through technical exercises — bass gymnastics if you will — keep in mind that music is *fun*. Make sure you assign a good chunk of time for playing songs or just "noodling"; it's important.

TIP

My suggestion is to divide your practice time into thirds. Dedicate the first third to the physical warm-ups; the second to scales, arpeggios, and other theoretical stuff; and the last third to consolidating the physical and theoretical workout into grooves and songs — or just noodling.

If you're able to practice for 30 minutes, start by warming up for 10 minutes with string crossing and finger exercises, then run scales and arpeggios for the next 10, and then play some fun stuff to fill out the final 10. If it's a 15-minute session, your increments are 5 minutes each. If you have exactly 23 minutes, then you may want to break out a calculator, or just wing it; don't take this suggested schedule *too* seriously.

The importance of noodling

How important is it to do some noodling on your instrument after you practice all those scales and arpeggios? Very. It's like playtime after your puppy's obedience training. You gotta have fun. Besides, you often find that you have the best musical ideas when you're just playing. *Noodling* — playing without any preconceived plan or goal — lets you get in touch with your creativity, a very important asset in a musician.

Simply let your fingers roam and see where they lead you. Don't worry about any of it making theoretical sense. Just discover what certain note combinations sound like, compose your very own groove, copy another groove you enjoy listening to, or even invent a whole new technique for playing bass.

Making a fool of yourself

When you practice, you want to be able to sound bad without passing harsh judgment on yourself. After all, you're practicing to get better; therefore, you practice things you still need to work on, right? So be kind to yourself, keep your mood light and your frustrations at bay, and get ready to play some really foolish stuff. It's fun. How do I know? Take a wild guess.

When you take music too seriously, you can really crimp your joy of playing. It's not that music shouldn't be taken seriously — of course it should, but not all the time. Keep a playful element in your playing.

Exercises for a lifetime

Playing bass is an art that takes constant practice. It's not as if you can quit playing a finger exercise after you finally master it. Your fingers would get rusty again pretty quickly. Don't you have to keep exercising your body in order to stay fit? That goes for your fingers, too.

Certain exercises in this book are sure to be in your personal practice routine for your entire bass-playing career. Others are exercises that you can revisit on a regular basis but that may not be part of your daily routine. Still others are useful for the occasional deviation from what you usually do, when you're just in the mood to play something different.

REMEMBER

None of the exercises in this book is a waste of practice time, but the "lifers" deserve your special attention. When I recommend that you play an exercise regularly, it may be a good idea for you to add it to your permanent practice routine.

Getting into Position

Having a nice, comfortable space to practice in — and even more important, *being* comfortable in that space — needs to be on top of your "bass-desires." Whether you sit or stand while practicing, you want to position your bass for your ease and comfort, so that your hands have complete access to the notes.

Your posture

TIP

I suggest always wearing a strap with your bass, regardless of whether you're standing or sitting. This ensures that your bass guitar is always in the same position, and you get used to finding your way on it in a consistent manner. You need to be able to reach all the strings with your striking hand (the hand that you strike the strings with, usually the right) and all the frets with your fretting hand (the hand you fret the notes with, usually the left).

Be very careful not to stare at the front of your fingerboard (the part of your bass's neck that holds the frets); your neck and wrists would be strained beyond comfort. Instead, look at the edge of the neck.

Keep your back straight, your shoulders wide, and your arms loose. Don't forget to breathe every once in a while. Whether you sit or stand, your bass should hang from your shoulders and rest firmly against your belly. If you'd like to review proper position and posture in detail, take a look at *Bass Guitar For Dummies*, 2nd Edition (Wiley).

Positioning your hands

Position your striking hand so that you can strike any string with minimal movement of your hand. In fact, I prefer to rest my thumb on a thumb rest or on the pickup. It gives me a great vantage point from which to measure the distance of each string by feel rather than having to look at it. This position is best for fingerstyle technique, which this book focuses on. Of course, if you're really comfortable with pick playing or with slapping, you may want to use that technique to get yourself through these exercises. For more details on alternate right-hand techniques, you can refer to *Bass Guitar For Dummies*, 2nd Edition.

You want to position your fretting hand to cover one fret per finger without causing any undue stress. By using one finger per fret, you set up your hand to execute by far the most musical figures with minimal (if any) shifting. In case you do have to shift, it's usually by one or two frets in either direction. This four-finger method gives your hand the consistency to play all patterns by feel rather than by vision.

Tackling Notation

Your bass guitar is the perfect instrument — perfectly symmetrical, gentle but authoritative in tone, expertly combining rhythm and harmony, and beautifully stating grooves as well as melodies.

An interesting peculiarity presents itself on bass (and other stringed instruments). Each note written for piano can be played in only one spot. Not so on your bass guitar. The same written note can be played in three or four different spots on your fingerboard. This is why positioning your hand correctly is so important in playing the exercises in this book.

Note names on the neck

Any scale and any arpeggio that you play on bass follows a precise pattern. The pattern never changes (except when using open strings). Only the starting point changes, dictated by the key. For instance, the C major scale feels exactly like the G major scale — both patterns are identical. The only difference is that you start the C major scale on C (at the 3rd fret on the A string) and the G major scale on G (at the 3rd fret on the E string). The following figure gives you a rundown of the names of the notes on your fingerboard. Note that they repeat at the 12th fret (the double-dot).

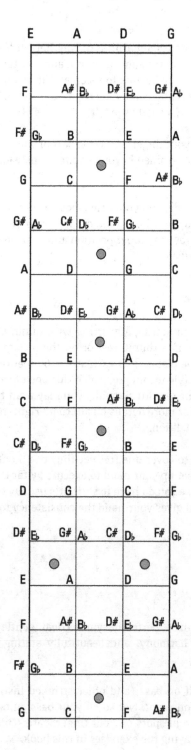

Traditional music notation and tablature

Throughout this book I combine traditional music notation with *tablature*, also called *tab*. Music notation shows you the note, octave, and rhythm of the desired tone, whereas tablature gives you the location on your bass guitar's fingerboard.

Tablature shows you what fret to press, and on which string, in order to get the desired note. The following two figures show you how the strings of your bass guitar correspond to the lines of the tablature staff and how the notes in music notation correspond to the frets on each string.

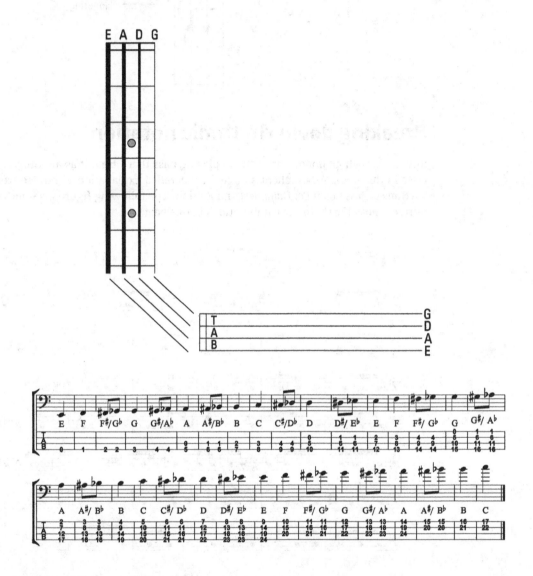

Using the grid

The grid represents the bass neck, looking at it head-on. I use the grid when I want you to see a pattern — for example, the shape of a scale or an arpeggio. You can visually remember the pattern; it doesn't change. The open circle represents the root of a scale or chord, and the black dots are the scale and chord tones. Take a look at the next figure to see the different parts of a grid.

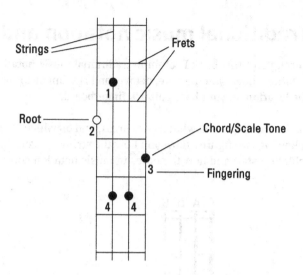

Breaking down rhythmic notation

Rhythm is such an important factor in playing bass that I treat it as an integral part of the exercises in this book. An excellent source for a detailed explanation of how to work with different rhythms is *Bass Guitar For Dummies*, 2nd Edition. The following figure gives you a rundown of the different possible rhythmic combinations in one beat.

The next figure shows you how notes that last longer than one beat are represented in music notation.

As the following figure shows, you can also *tie* one note to the next, thus extending its length by adding both notes together.

Chord notation

TIP

The idea behind chord notation: write a little, describe a lot. Instead of writing "Use the Mixolydian mode on C and outline a dominant tonality with the root, 3rd, 5th, and flat 7th," you can instead simply sum it all up as "C7."

You can extract two types of information from a chord symbol: the chord tones of the harmony and the scale tones of the mode. The following figure gives you examples of some of the most commonly used chord symbols, along with the corresponding chord tones and modes.

REMEMBER

Occasionally you encounter chord symbols that use numbers other than 7 — 6, 9, 11, or 13. Treat any chord that doesn't have a major or minor symbol in front of the number as a dominant chord and use the Mixolydian mode with it, with one exception. If the number is 6, treat the chord as a major chord and use Ionian (note that you treat the C9, C11, and C13 exactly as you would the C7).

Chapter **2**

Warming Up Your Right and Left Hands

D o you know that feeling when it's time to get up after a much-too-short night of sleep, and you stumble to the bathroom, trying not to knock over everything that's not bolted down? That's what your fingers feel like when you first pick up the bass for your daily practice routine.

Warming up is a form of waking up to the task at hand, whether it's an athletic activity or playing a musical instrument. To play at the height of your ability, you first want to take your hands through all the motions you encounter when playing bass.

This chapter leads you through the moves your hands need to make in order to be in full control of your instrument, whether it's crossing the strings with your right hand, shifting with your left, or employing individual finger independence. A warm-up doesn't have to sound pretty; it's for getting the stumble out of your fingers. You certainly sound a lot better after a proper warm-up.

Stretching without the Instrument

Developing strong fingers and a strong back keeps you in optimum shape and gives you the endurance to play for hours without getting cramps or getting fatigued. You also want to be comfortable carrying the weight of the bass on your shoulders while still moving your arms comfortably.

Here are some exercises to get you started before you even touch your bass.

Getting a feel for each finger

Developing your fingers is a top priority for playing bass. You want to keep your fingers curved and playing on the fingertips without the knuckles collapsing. What do fingers in proper playing position feel like?

Take the thumb and index finger of your left hand and press the tips lightly together, as if you're flashing someone an "OK" sign (see Figure 2-1). Now increase the pressure on the tips. You can feel how the knuckles want to collapse, but don't let them. Maintain the shape of the "O," and keep all the joints in your fingers well-rounded. After holding the index finger and the thumb pressed together for about 20 seconds, release them and repeat this same exercise with your middle finger and thumb, followed by your ring finger and then your pinkie. After completing this exercise with your left hand, repeat it with your right.

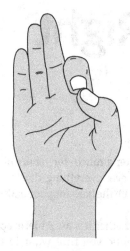

FIGURE 2-1: Pressing the fingers to the thumb.

Stretching your hands

A muscle can only contract; it can't stretch on its own. In order to keep your muscles limber and loose, you need to stretch them out every once in a while.

Put your right and left hands together, palm to palm, finger to finger, as if you were praying (see Figure 2-2). Then spread your fingers wide while keeping your hands firmly together. Keep them spread, and gently bring your elbows up while keeping your hands at chest level. Your wrists should end up at about a 90-degree angle to your arms. Hold this position for about 20 seconds, and then release.

Getting blood into your fingertips

One of the worst moves you can make with your hands is to shake them as if you've hit your finger with a hammer while nailing a picture of your favorite bassist on the wall. Shaking your hands from the wrist can do some serious damage. A much more gentle and effective method of "shaking" is the "flick."

FIGURE 2-2:
Keeping the
hands together.

Imagine you're flicking something off the tip of your thumb with your index finger. That's kind of the motion you're going for in this exercise, which is illustrated in Figure 2-3. Make a very loose fist by angling your thumb against your fingernails. Press the fingers against your thumb as they try to straighten, and finally, let them flick past the thumb.

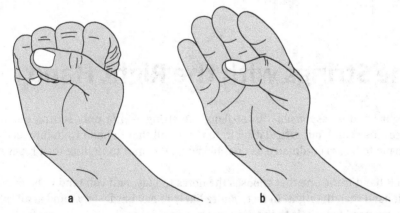

FIGURE 2-3:
Fingers
behind thumb (a)
and then
pastthumb (b).

Stretching your shoulders and your back

Your average bass guitar weighs between 7 and 11 pounds, and if that doesn't sound like much initially, you feel a lot less happy about those pounds after a four-hour jam with no breaks. Before subjecting your shoulders and your back to the weight of your bass, stretch them out.

Lift your right arm straight up, and then bend your elbow until your hand comes to rest between your shoulder blades. It's almost as if you're trying to scratch an itch in the middle of your back. Next, bring your left hand behind your back at your waistline, and reach up to touch your right hand. If you're flexible enough, you can grasp the fingers of your right hand with those of your left. If you're not, dangle a strap from your right hand and grasp it with the left (see Figure 2-4). Hold this position for about 20 seconds (don't forget to breathe), and then repeat the exercise in reverse — left on top, right on bottom.

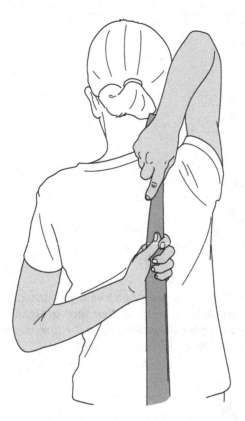

FIGURE 2-4:
Using a strap to join hands behind the back.

Crossing the Strings with the Right Hand

The right hand is responsible for striking the string — not only setting off the vibration that produces the sound, but articulating it, too. With all that in hand (pun intended), you want your right hand to be as coordinated as possible when it comes to finding the proper string.

Your left hand is the one that chooses the notes to play, and you tend to be much more aware of the left hand than the right. In fact, you're likely to pay hardly any mind at all to the right, which means you need to train it to function on its own.

Alternating up and raking down

In playing fingerstyle, the right-hand concept for crossing strings is pretty straightforward. As the following figure shows, when you travel from the low to the high strings, you alternate between the index and middle fingers in striking the string. When traveling from the high to the low strings, you strike with the same finger. This exercise knocks your right hand into shape in no time. Pay very close attention to the right-hand finger combinations, as they're key to this exercise.

Referencing each string

Naturally, you won't always go straight up and down the strings of your bass. In fact, very often you find yourself coming back to the same string. This next exercise helps you maintain the discipline of alternating your right-hand fingers on the way up and raking with the same finger on the way down, no matter how many strings are in play. Again, pay very close attention to the right-hand fingering in the following figure, and take it slowly at first. The speed comes later — no worries.

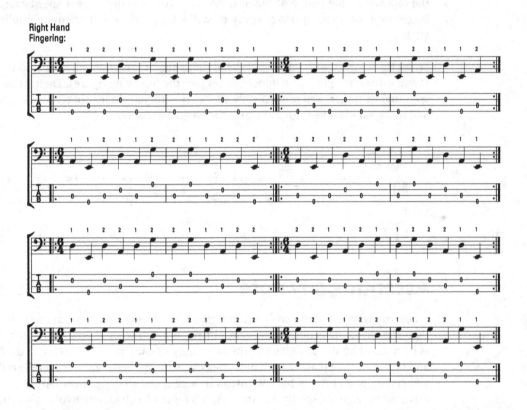

In both of the previous exercises, you don't use your left hand at all; the exercises are played on the open strings. In this way you can really hone in on the right-hand finger combinations. These are far from the prettiest exercises, so keep your volume kind of low.

Exercising One String at a Time

When you strike a string, you want to have control of several key things: speed, note duration, accents, and dynamics. All these factors are controlled largely by your right hand. The following exercises help you develop the skills to exercise some intricate details with your right hand.

Again, leave the left hand out of it. This is purely a workout for the right. The strings are vibrating freely, so keep your volume down.

Striking the staccato way

Staccato means *detached*. Instead of letting a note ring until you strike the next one, stop the vibration of the string, and silence the note before playing another. Believe it or not, despite the relatively slow tempo of the next exercise, it's actually a great speed exercise, as you have to get your alternating finger ready to strike the next note immediately following the initial strike.

Strike the E string with your right-hand index finger, and immediately stop the vibration of the string with your right-hand middle finger (see the following figure). Then strike the E string with your middle finger, and immediately silence it with your index finger. Repeat this on all strings, and make sure you keep an even space between each note.

Accenting any note

When you want a note to stick out in a crowd (of notes), you want to *accent* it, or play it louder than the others. This may sound easy at first, but you soon realize how much of Western music is dominated by the downbeat at the beginning of each measure. Refer to the following figure, and take your time playing each note, especially the in-between notes on the offbeats. Make sure you clearly accent the notes you intend to accent (by striking them harder), and play the non-accented notes more lightly. Sometimes, it's more of a challenge to play the quiet notes than the accented ones.

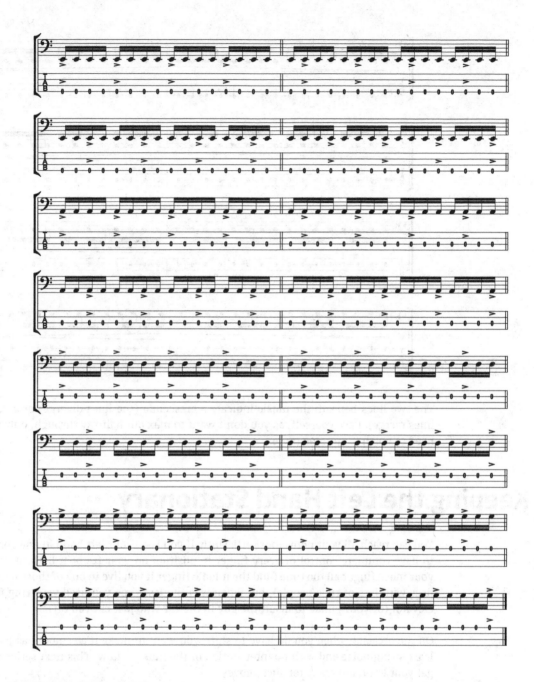

Using dynamics

The official term for music that gets gradually louder or softer is *crescendo* or *decrescendo* (respectively). As a bass player, part of your job is to keep the rhythm steady. It's no easy task to hold a steady beat when you also have to build the musical phrase to an eardrum-shattering crescendo (or bring it down to a whisper). The challenge in the following exercise is to keep the tempo rock-steady as you manipulate the volume *(dynamics)* of the notes. You *must* use a metronome with this exercise; without it, you can't be sure your speed is constant.

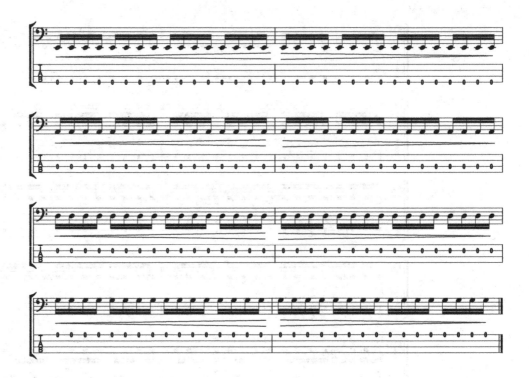

The two lines beneath the music indicate a crescendo (the lines diverge) or a decrescendo (the lines merge). Pace yourself, as you don't want to max out halfway through, only to find that you need to notch it up some more.

Keeping the Left Hand Stationary

You can reach all your notes most efficiently if you keep your left hand in one position. You want to have complete control of every finger in position on your fretboard. Think about it. You use your index finger all the time (and the middle finger if you live in one of those dynamic metropolises with lots of rude people), but when was the last time you used your ring finger to call an elevator (or your pinkie to insult the guy in the car who just cut you off)?

On the occasion when you do have to shift, you want to make it as smooth as possible, with the least string noise and with no interruption of the music's flow. This next series of exercises can get your left hand ready for such moves.

Left-hand permutations

REMEMBER

The following exercise is, in all likelihood, one of the most important exercises you can ever learn, a definite "lifer." You can feel your hand getting into a whole new mode of proficiency after completing this series. Left-hand permutations give you all the possible finger combinations you encounter in one position. The following figures (*a* and *b*) show how to play the exercise on the lowest four frets, but be sure to move it to other areas of your fingerboard after you have a handle on it.

(a)

(b)

Walking spider

The wonderful bassist John Patitucci made part of this following exercise — the *walking spider* — a household name among bassists. Your left hand has to feel where the strings are without your looking directly at the fingerboard. In addition, you need to keep your notes even and balanced, no matter what string you're playing on. You can see that the leaps are pretty significant, so take it slowly at first. Also, make sure you keep your left hand loose; don't overstretch. The right hand may struggle at first to strike all the right strings, but with a little practice you can gain fabulous benefits from this exercise.

Getting a buzz

How misleading a heading can be, eh? This isn't about anything but playing bass. This exercise helps you determine how much pressure it takes to get a good note out of your instrument, and it was largely developed by the excellent bass player Gary Willis. Referring to the following figure, you slowly press the E string down at the 1st fret while striking the string with the right hand. As your left-hand finger approaches the fret, the string starts to buzz. The string begins to buzz just before you put enough pressure on it to get a clean note. After you get the buzz, increase the pressure on the string incrementally, until the sound is clean and clear. Go back and forth between buzz and clean note to learn how little pressure is necessary to produce the note. Do this with all fingers on all strings, and feel how your left hand lightens up as a result.

Cutting down on excess finger movement

For speed and dexterity, you want to play your bass with as little excess motion as possible, especially from your left-hand fingers. If you find that your fingers are flying off the fretboard instead of staying close to the string, the following dead-note exercise is great for keeping them close and ready for action. The less distance you put between your fingers and the string, the faster they're able to return to the string to play the next note. (When you watch really good bass players, you can hardly see what notes they're playing; their fingers seem not to move at all.) In this exercise, the notes are played in triplets (the fingers of the right hand alternate in striking the notes), and they're strategically placed so that you can check whether you're doing the exercise properly.

All the notes in this exercise are played on the 5th fret on open strings. Play the first note of each triplet so it rings out clearly, using the assigned finger. Staying in the same position, play the next two notes as dead notes by lightly resting all your left-hand fingers on the string at the same time to mute it. Don't let the string reach the fretboard anywhere. If done properly, you get a dead thud; if only one finger touches it, you hear an annoying harmonic. This trains your fingers to keep close by and leads to your playing with much more ease and efficiency. Of course, you won't be as exciting to watch on a music video, but you'll sound great.

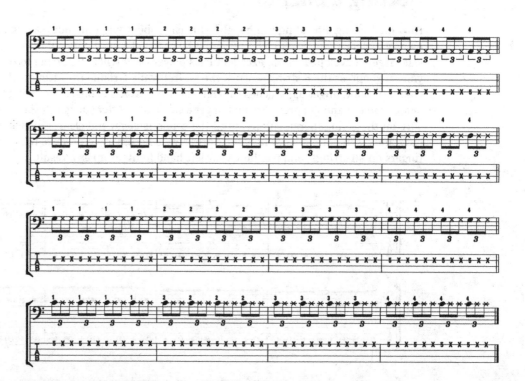

Shifting the Left Hand

A key skill for any successful bass player is to be able to reach any note in an instant along the entire fingerboard. Shifting smoothly and accurately with the left hand allows you to play a wide array of note combinations.

Of course, nothing is worse than shifting in search of just the right note and ending up with a really annoying hiss from the motion of the fingers on the strings. The exercises in this section help you coordinate the left-hand movement flawlessly.

Shifting with any finger

You never know which finger you'll end up using at the end of a musical phrase, so it's a good idea to be prepared to shift with any finger. The following series of exercises helps you develop good shifting habits for any finger. By far, most of your shifts are one- or two-fret shifts. Therefore, these exercises concentrate on "close-quarters" movements. Play them with a metronome, because you don't want to slow down or speed up when shifting into a new position. Each little segment starts on the click and ends on the click.

In the following figures, the ascending, one-fret-shifting exercise is followed by the ascending, two-fret-shifting exercise.

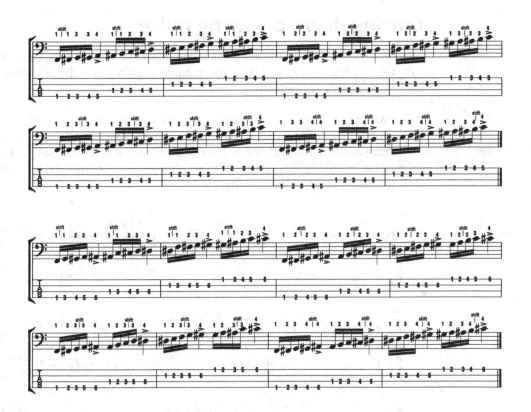

Of course, you can't just keep shifting up — you need to be able to get down as well. The following figures show the one-fret-shifting exercise coming down, followed by the two-fret version descending.

Cutting down on string noise

When you move your left hand along the string to get to a new position, you want to minimize the sound of your fingers scraping along the string by slightly lifting them off. You can train your left hand by doing this next exercise.

Referring to the following figure, play the 4th fret of each string with a different finger. This gives you a chance to tell whether all your notes sound even. Your hand has to shift into a new position each time you use a different finger. Listen for any string noise, and keep it to a minimum. This exercise isn't easy, but the good news is that after you have control of this movement, every other shift is a piece of cake, comparatively.

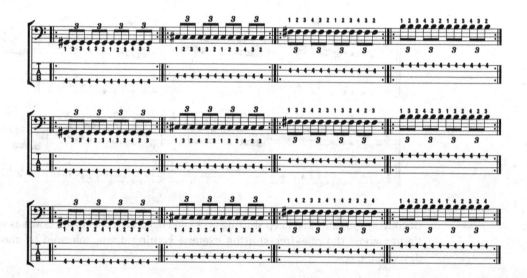

2

Scales (Modes) and Chords

Scales: They're not just for fish anymore. In fact, this part shows you some really cool ways to make this backbone of music to be your new best friend. They're a great workout partner for your hands to boot. You discover how to combine scales and chords, how to resolve them rhythmically, and most important, how to apply all this new information to real music. After all, that's why you practice in the first place, right?

Chapter **3**

Playing Scales (Modes)

Most music is based on *scales*, which are also called *modes*. By memorizing scale patterns, you can have all kinds of musical phrases at your fingertips — literally.

Each kind of scale consists of a unique pattern of notes on your fingerboard, and each is consistent, no matter what fret you start on. The trick to developing speed and fluidity in your bass playing is to practice each mode repeatedly until your hand recognizes the pattern without your having to think much about it.

In this chapter, you discover the best fingering for the most commonly used scales. As a bass player, one of your primary responsibilities is to provide the groove for a song. To do so effectively, you have to be able to reach any note in the scale pattern related to that groove's tonality. Your groove usually works well within one octave (root to root), so you need to be very comfortable playing each note in that octave. After you work your way through these exercises, you can apply your newfound skill to real music at the end of this chapter.

REMEMBER

It's all about the pattern. As you memorize each of the scales, you can simply start the pattern of that scale anywhere on your fingerboard and know that it never changes, whether you start on C, F, or any other key.

Playing the Primary Modes

The four most commonly used chords in music are major, minor, dominant, and half-diminished. You want to first concentrate on practicing the modal patterns that coincide with the harmony of these chords. The four modes that fit best over them are called Ionian, Dorian, Mixolydian, and Locrian. Sounds fancy, right? Your mission, should you choose to accept it, is to memorize the pattern of each of these four modes and the chord it's linked with.

Using your fretting hand, you start the major and dominant modes (Ionian and Mixolydian) with your second finger and the minor and half-diminished modes (Dorian and Locrian) with your index finger. You can begin the scales on either the E or A string, and remember that these scales are meant to be moved around the neck. Try starting them on different frets, each of which represents a different key.

Throughout this book, I present each scale pattern as a neck diagram, as well as in music notation and in tab; each exercise is shown in music notation and tab. You can use any figure as a reference, because the objective here is to get you comfortable with the pattern.

Major scale — Ionian

The major scale is also known by its formal name, the *Ionian mode,* and is used for — oh, wait, let me guess — yes, the major chord (see the following figure). Start this scale using your second finger on either the E or the A string and let 'er rip! You may find it very useful to memorize the fingering pattern first to help you through this scale. This one has no shifts — simply start with your second finger and follow the pattern.

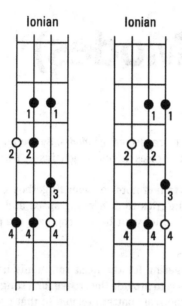

Check out the following figure for Ionian fingering, musical notation, and tab. Notice how the scale always starts on either the E or A string. (You need three strings to complete the scale without shifting.)

The most efficient way to make the Ionian mode (or any mode, for that matter) your own is to play its pattern, beginning on any fret of the E or A string, and then to shift it up or down by one fret at a time. For example, play the scale starting on B, then C, and so on. This re- inforces the pattern for your fingers rather than your having to worry about note names. See the following figure for fingering for 12 ascending major scales, in music notation and tab.

After you have a solid handle on this exercise, try the same scale *descending*, starting on the highest note and going to the lowest note (see the following figure). This time your Ionian mode starts on the G or D string. Again, work this scale under your fingers by shifting it one fret at a time.

TRACK 1, 0:11

When you're comfortable with the descending scale, combine ascending and descending and start them on different frets along the fingerboard. The following figure has fingering for the 12 ascending and descending major scales in music notation and tab.

Repetition and consistency are the all-important ingredients to becoming completely comfortable with the scale patterns, so keep at it.

Minor scale — Dorian

The Dorian mode is especially important for bass players. Two different minor scales, the Dorian and the Aeolian modes, are used in playing, and for different purposes. The *Dorian mode* is primarily played in minor grooves and single-chord solos and fills. Because the bass is a groove instrument, the Dorian mode is your primary minor scale. The *Aeolian mode* (also called the *natural minor scale*) is used when playing melodies in a minor key.

Take a look at the grid and the music in the following figure. Note that you begin the scale with your index finger. Of the seven different scales in this chapter, the Dorian mode is the only one requiring a shift, albeit a very small one. After playing on the lower two strings in position, you need to shift your fretting hand toward the headstock by one fret and play the subsequent note with your index finger.

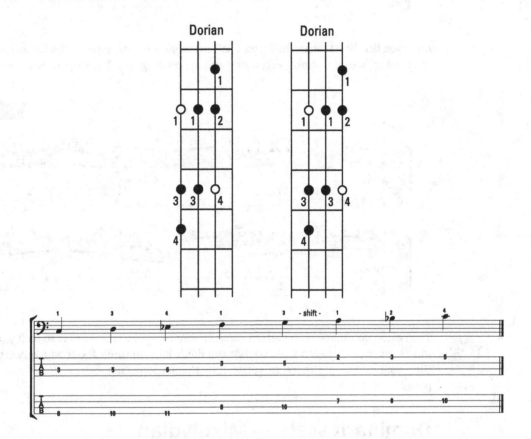

Play the Dorian mode in every position by moving the entire pattern from one end of your fingerboard to the other, one fret at a time. Always start the pattern on the E or A string when you're playing an ascending scale (see the following figure).

TRACK 1, 0:45

When you're comfortable with the ascending Dorian mode, play it descending, starting with your pinkie on the G or D string (see the next figure).

TRACK 1, 0:56

A-Dorian   B♭-Dorian   B-Dorian   C-Dorian

After you firmly establish the Dorian pattern in your hands, refer to the following figure and play the scale in both directions, ascending and descending, moving the pattern one fret at a time.

TRACK 1, 1:07

A-Dorian   B♭-Dorian

B-Dorian   C-Dorian

TIP

The reason you move each pattern *chromatically* (one fret at a time) is to lock your hand into the muscle memory for each scale so that you don't have to think about which notes you're playing. Give your hands a chance to settle into the pattern first before doing any more advanced patterns.

Dominant scale — Mixolydian

The *dominant scale*, or *Mixolydian mode*, is the most commonly used scale for bass grooves. You can think of it as a major scale with a lowered seventh. Like every "major-ish" scale, you start this pattern using your middle finger. Get your fingers (and ears) familiar with this pattern; no shifts are necessary or desired. The following figure shows the fingering for the Mixolydian mode in neck diagram, music notation, and tab.

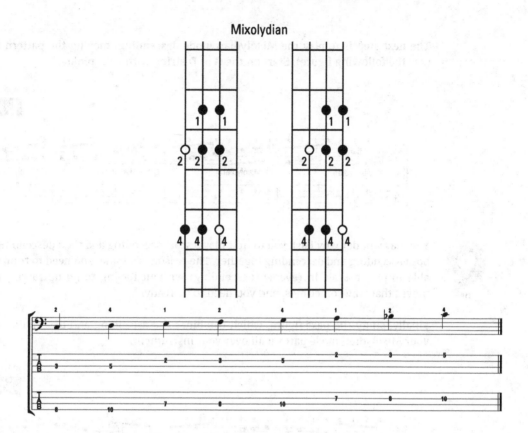

Mixolydian

After you have the ascending Mixolydian scale under your fingers, shift it all over your finger-board by moving it from one fret to the next (see the following figure). Always start on the E or A string.

TRACK 1, 1:30

A-Mixolydian   B♭-Mixolydian   B-Mixolydian   C-Mixolydian

The next step is to play the Mixolydian mode descending, moving the pattern from fret to fret (see the following figure). Start on the G or D string with your pinkie.

TRACK 1, 1:42

TIP

You may wonder why I ask you to first play a scale ascending and then descending, before putting both ascending and descending together. The reason is simple. You need to train your hands to be able to play a scale in reverse (descending) without having to go up (ascending) first. Music moves that way sometimes, and you need to be ready.

Finally, study the next figure, which combines the ascending and descending moves, and play your Mixolydian mode pattern all over your instrument.

TRACK 1, 1:54

There, now don't you feel dominant?

Half-diminished scale — Locrian

The unique sound of the half-diminished is a minor with a lowered fifth, and the scale to play over it is the *Locrian mode* (which also includes a flatted second and flatted sixth). Start this scale with your index finger on the E or A string. No shifting is necessary; just get your fingers used to the proper position and your ears to the dissonant sound of it. You know the drill — get to know your pattern. The following figure shows the fingering for the Locrian mode in neck diagram, music notation, and tab.

Locrian

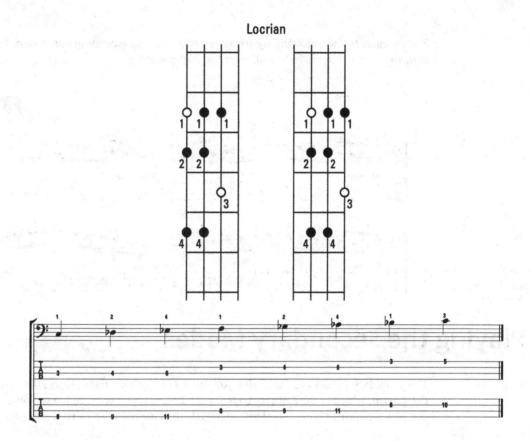

When you have a solid grip (pun intended) on the pattern, move it all over the fingerboard, one fret at a time, and always start each scale with your index finger on the E or A string as you play the ascending Locrian mode (see the following figure).

TRACK 1, 2:17

Now play the same scale descending. Move it all over the fingerboard, one fret at a time, starting on the G or D string with your ring finger (see the following figure).

TRACK 1, 2:29

Finally, refer to the following figure as you combine the ascending and descending Locrian mode and, you guessed it, move 'em all over the fingerboard.

TRACK 1, 2:40

Playing the Secondary Modes

The secondary modes are the scales you use less often as a bass player, because of the nature of the groove (which is the primary bass focus). Even so, you want to know these scales well so you can play smoothly through melodic material, such as melodies or riffs and fills.

The secondary scales are the *Phrygian mode*, the *Aeolian mode* (also called the *natural minor scale*), and the *Lydian mode*. They work very well as connecting tissue between the primary modes. You get to play them as a connecting function a little later in this chapter, but for now it's time to make them your own.

Phrygian — The exotic minor scale

The *Phrygian mode* fits over a minor chord but adds a bit of an exotic flavor to the mix. Familiarize yourself with the following pattern, and get used to the somewhat unusual sound.

Phrygian

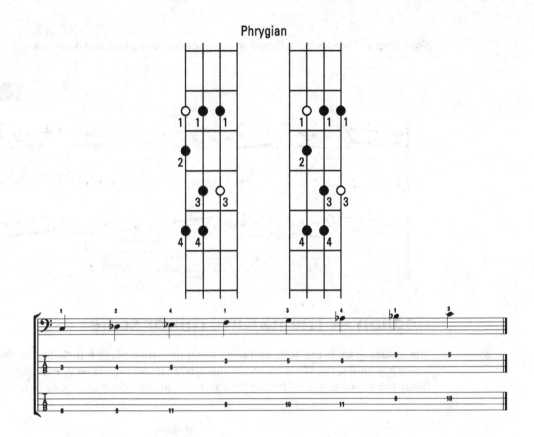

Move the Phrygian all over the fingerboard. Practice this scale by playing it ascending and then descending (see the following figure).

Now, refer to the following figure as you combine ascending and descending.

TRACK 1, 3:27

Aeolian — The natural minor scale

The *Aeolian mode* is the scale you most often use when playing melodies in songs that are in a minor key. Unlike the Phrygian mode, the Aeolian mode sounds very, well, natural. The following figure shows the fingering for the Aeolian mode in neck diagram, music notation, and tab.

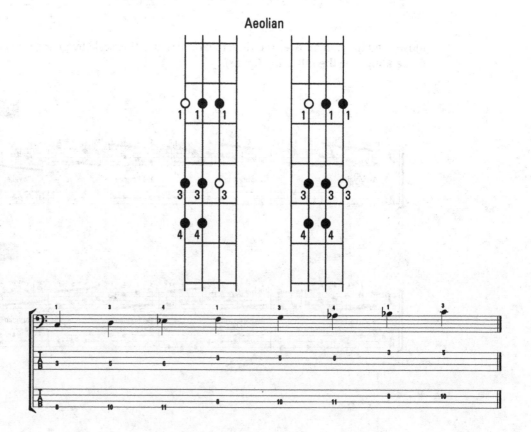

Play the ascending Aeolian mode and move it one fret at a time, starting on either the E or A string (see the next figure).

TRACK 1, 3:50

Do the same with the descending scale (refer to the following figure).

TRACK 1, 4:02

Finally, combine the ascending and descending Aeolian mode (see the next figure).

TRACK 1, 4:14

Lydian — Major scale with a twang

The *Lydian mode* is a major scale with a bit of an edge. Get the pattern under your fingers before moving it anywhere else. The following figure shows the fingering for the Lydian mode in neck diagram, music notation, and tab.

Lydian

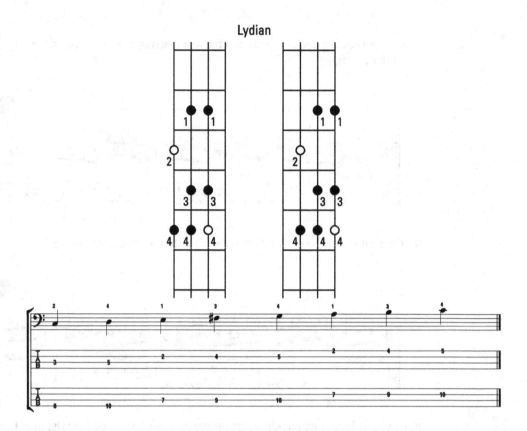

Now, move the pattern all over your fingerboard. Be sure to keep your fingering consistent. Refer to the following figures as you go up, down, and then combine the two.

TRACK 1, 4:36

Making Music

It's time to use your modal knowledge to play a song. In the following piece, you can reach all your notes for the melody in one position. You can either play it down low in the bass range or take it up an octave (just follow either tablature). Wherever you decide to play this melody, it's based on the C Ionian mode. Start with your middle finger on the C of the A string and have fun with it.

Chapter **4**

Playing Mode Sequences

I f you've practiced the seven modes (scales) in Chapter 3 as diligently as I think you have, you're now ready to combine the major and minor scales in various sequences. *Sequences* are standard musical patterns that use notes from the modes; they give a musical piece enough predictability to make it memorable, but not so much as to make it boring.

The advantage of practicing sequences is that it prepares your fretting hand to move quickly into the optimal position to reach a large range of related notes. And, of course, they sound musical. It's so much easier to practice something you actually enjoy listening to.

In this chapter, I introduce some major and minor sequences. These interval exercises give you practice in skipping notes in the scale. After you're comfortable with the sequences, you're ready to let loose with the progressive rock music at the end of the chapter.

Lining Up Major and Minor Sequences in 12 Keys

Modes always line up in a certain sequence. If you're playing in a major key, the sequence starts with the Ionian mode and is followed by the Dorian, Phrygian, Lydian, Mixolydian, Aeolian, and Locrian modes.

On the other hand, if you're playing in a minor key, you begin the same modal sequence starting with the Aeolian mode, followed by the Locrian, Ionian, Dorian, Phrygian, Lydian, and Mixolydian modes.

Getting into the majors

Skip the major speeches and get down to these major exercises in the major sequence for you major players (not a minor matter).

The basic major scale sequence

The exercise in the following figure simply lines up all your modes from Chapter 3 in sequence. Observe the fingering and the shifts — they're indicated above the notes. You shift into position for each scale.

Though this alignment of related scales looks pretty useless for learning how to play in a band, practicing the following exercise is very important and practical. It gets your fingers and ears ready to respond with the correct note choices related to the key of the musical piece you're playing.

REMEMBER Even though I present you with only one key in this example, you can, and should, play this sequence in every key. Only in the keys of E and F do you have to resort to using open strings (and thus to using a different initial pattern). All other keys follow the exact same pattern; just start on the appropriate fret for each key.

The following example is in the key of G major, ascending.

The beginning of the sequence looks a little different in the keys of E and F major (see the following two figures).

What goes up must come down. The next figure shows the descending version of the G major modal sequence exercise.

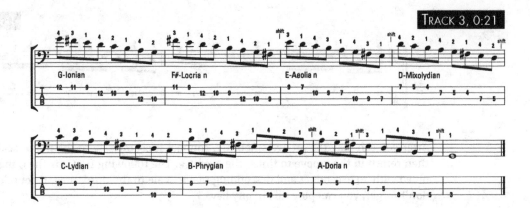

Listen carefully to what you're playing. This is a great ear-training exercise as well as a great finger workout.

Major scale sequence — scale sequence to the third

The next exercise provides you with ample opportunity to practice crossing strings while playing a major scale sequence. The sequence in the following figure — ascending C major scale to the third — is often used in musical pieces.

TRACK 4, 0:00

As always, move this pattern through all 12 keys; it's compact enough that you don't even have to worry about open strings — or shifts, for that matter. The descending C major scale sequence appears in the next figure.

TRACK 4, 0:09

Do you notice how nicely this exercise resolves rhythmically? Rhythm is an essential part of playing bass, and you now get to connect this pattern to a C major groove, shown in the next figure, to make some cool music. In a band, the bass player virtually never stops playing. The groove you play with this major scale outlines the same major tonality. Practice the groove first before connecting it to the scale.

After you can play the groove smoothly, connect it seamlessly to the major scale sequence, and then return to the groove to finish the exercise. The following figure is the C major groove combined with an ascending and descending major scale to the third. Alas, it sounds like music! And don't forget, you can play this in any key.

TRACK 5

Major scale sequence — scale in fifths

A similar exercise to the preceding one is the next sequence, using an interval of a fifth to start the line. It shifts out of position and sounds much more far-flung. Check out the following two figures — an ascending C major scale in fifths and a descending C major scale in fifths.

Notice that the groove that connects the ascending and descending segments is the same one you use in the preceding exercise. When you put it all together, you get the little beauty in the following figure (watch out for the shifts).

Move the exercise through all 12 keys and feel the blood pumping through your fingers. Make sure you keep the shifts consistent.

Practicing minor sequences

So that the minor matter of the minor tonality isn't a major obstacle, here's a selection of minor patterns for a major workout.

The basic minor scale sequence

It's time to line up your modes in a minor key. The good news is that the overall sequence is exactly the same for both the minor and major modes. The only difference is that you start the minor mode sequence from the root of the Aeolian and then line the modes up from there: from Aeolian to Locrian, Ionian, Dorian, Phrygian, Lydian, Mixolydian, and back to Aeolian (see Chapter 3 for more on these modes).

REMEMBER

The example in the following figure is in the key of G, but you can use this same pattern in all 12 keys by moving it to the appropriate fret. Only in the key of E do you have to change the initial pattern to an open-string pattern. All other keys follow the exact same pattern; they just start on different frets.

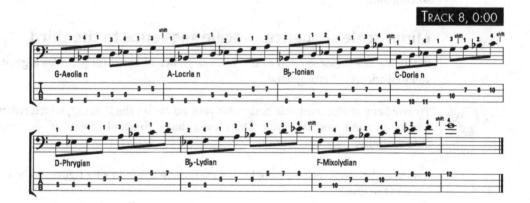

The beginning of the ascending sequence looks a little different in the key of E minor, as shown in the next figure.

The following figure shows the descending segment of this exercise.

Listen carefully to the sound of the sequence to give your ears a workout while your fingers are slaving away.

Minor scale sequence — scale sequence to the third

Practicing the minor version of the scale sequence to the third provides a great opportunity for you to work your fretting hand.

To avoid any shifts, start this scale with your pinkie on the E string, which twists your hand into perfect fretting position. You don't even have to think about it — your hand does it automatically.

Carefully check out the fingering for the exercise in the following figure — the ascending C minor scale to the third.

Move this pattern through all 12 keys. It's compact enough to be played without shifting or resorting to open strings. The next figure shows the descending sequence.

TRACK 9, 0:09

Listen to how this exercise rhythmically resolves, just like its major counterpart. When you add a C minor groove to this, you can move seamlessly between the scale and the groove. The groove you play in this exercise outlines a minor tonality and looks like the next figure.

TRACK 9, 0:20

Work on this groove until you can play it smoothly. Then practice connecting it seamlessly to the minor scale sequence and finally returning to the groove to finish the whole thing.

REMEMBER

Note, however, that you need to shift between the groove position and the scale position — and it's quite a shift. You can't start this exercise below the 4th fret of the E string. Pay close attention to the shifting move in the next figure.

Practice this in all keys following the pattern. Enjoy — it's a very useful exercise for real-life playing.

Minor scale sequence — scale in fifths

The following two figures show the ascending and descending C minor scale in fifths.

REMEMBER

Playing the minor version of the scale in fifths requires you to reposition your fretting hand; start this sequence with the index finger on the E string. Note the shift right at the beginning and be ready for it. Follow the fingering in the chart and take your time getting the feel of this; it can be very tricky.

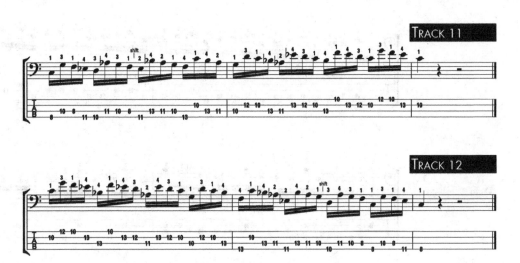

The groove that connects the ascending and descending segments, shown in the next figure, is the same one you use in the preceding exercise. The shift feels slightly different, however, because your hand is positioned farther up the fingerboard. Pay close attention to the fingering for the shifts, and take your time. The best part, besides this being an extraordinary exercise for your hands, is that you can play it in any key.

Playing Sequences in Triplet Rhythm

A cool way to vary the rhythm is to play a scale sequence in *triplets* (three equal notes in one beat). In this section, you play both major and minor scale sequences with triplets, gradually increasing the distance between notes.

Major scale sequence — triplets and seconds

The following figure is an ascending C major sequence that uses the interval of the second with a triplet rhythm.

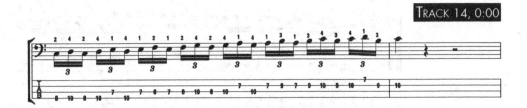

The next figure shows the descending version.

Wait a minute — is that a rhythmic resolution I hear? Oh, yeah! Well, in that case, add a nice little groove to the exercise and get the full benefit of playing bass.

The groove to use is, of course, a C major groove in triplets, and this one sounds kind of bluesy. The following two figures show the groove with the root on top and then the groove with the root on the bottom.

Putting it all together should be a breeze — well, maybe. Connecting these exercises to grooves takes them beyond the realm of exercise and into the world of real music.

REMEMBER

Play this exercise in all keys to get the most benefit from the workout.

Major scale sequence — triplets and thirds

Using the same triplet rhythm, you can play intervals of thirds. The distance between the notes is a bit larger, but the concept is the same. The following figure shows the ascending C major sequence in triplets.

The next figure gives the descending C major sequence in triplets and thirds.

And in the following figure you use the same groove from the previous exercises — which you've practiced diligently, right?

Would you like to venture a guess as to how many keys I'd like you to play this exercise in? All of them? You're quite right.

Major scale sequence — triplets and fifths

The final major sequence in this study of intervals features the fifths. This exercise makes use of the same triplet rhythm and groove from the previous two sections. This time, however, you need to prepare yourself for a shift within the sequence. In the next two figures, which show the ascending and descending sequences, follow the fingering very carefully and be consistent in all keys.

TRACK 18, 0:00

TRACK 18, 0:06

Now, check out the next figure and connect the exercises to the groove for the rhythmic resolution.

Play this exercise in all keys, please — and enjoy!

Minor scale sequence — triplets and seconds

The minor version of the triplet-rhythm scale sequence follows the same concept as the major version, but you put your fretting hand in a minor scale position. Start with your pinkie on the E string as you play the exercises in the following two figures — an ascending and a descending C minor sequence in triplets.

And now, to add the groove to the sequence and rhythmically resolve it, reposition your fretting hand to play the triplet groove with the root on top as it appears in the following figure.

Now play it with the root on the bottom, as in the next figure.

TRACK 20, 0:19

Finally, combine the groove with the sequence in the exercise and you create a beautiful combination that properly prepares you to play great music. As you play the sequence in the following figure, watch the shifts into and out of the groove, and follow the fingering diligently.

TRACK 21

As always, the key to success is . . . all keys.

Minor scale sequence — triplets and thirds

It's time to increase the distance between the notes. This next sequence of exercises works on your thirds in a minor scale. Your hand remains in the same position, with your pinkie on the root. The following two figures show the ascending and descending C minor sequence in triplets and thirds.

TRACK 22, 0:00

The next figure inserts the same groove from the previous sections. Make sure you observe the shift and the proper fingering.

REMEMBER

Move the exercise around at will, all over the fingerboard, while keeping the pattern consistent.

Minor scale sequence — triplets and fifths

Then there's that rather large interval, the fifth. It's too important an interval to ignore, so buckle down and get ready to tackle the fifth in triplets. You need to position your fretting hand to start the sequence with the index finger on the E string and to prepare yourself for a shift right at the beginning. See the following two figures for the ascending and descending sequences.

Now, connect the sequence to the groove for the rhythmic resolution. Watch out for the shift, and keep in mind that you have two grooves — one with the root on top, the other with the root on the bottom.

After you have a solid handle on it, please move it to all the other keys.

String Crossings with Interval Exercises

A great way to practice the string-crossing motion for playing grooves on bass is to practice interval exercises. These exercises help you locate any interval in relation to the scale's root. When you play grooves, you often leap from one note to the next, skipping the in-between notes that make it sound like a scale.

The following exercises help develop your hands so that you're able to play large intervals without losing track of the scale's root. Crossing the strings is the trickiest part of this, so the benefits of these exercises are knowing the intervals you're playing and being able to maneuver through the harmony without having to play every note in the scale.

Major scale sequence — referencing the root

In this exercise you get into position for the major scale and play the root, followed by each of the scale tones, one at a time; you're referencing the root between each note. The following figure shows the ascending sequence.

Just in case you like playing grooves with the root on top (and who doesn't on occasion), the next figure shows the descending part of this exercise.

Wow, that's some string-crossing, isn't it? You can see that this exercise is as much a workout for your right hand as it is for your left.

Minor scale sequence — referencing the root

Here's the minor version of the exercise.

REMEMBER

You need to keep your hand in groove-playing position, which means you start the sequence on the E or A string with your index finger. One small shift is required — you know the deal with the Dorian mode.

The next two figures show the ascending and descending sequences.

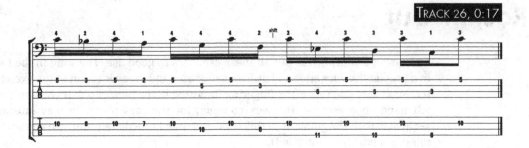

This exercise is a real workout for the shift, as well as for the fingering, isn't it? It's well worth the effort, though.

Dominant scale sequence — referencing the root

This is a groove exercise series, so there's no way the dominant scale can be ignored. The following two figures show the ascending and descending Mixolydian sequence, referencing the root.

TRACK 26, 0:22

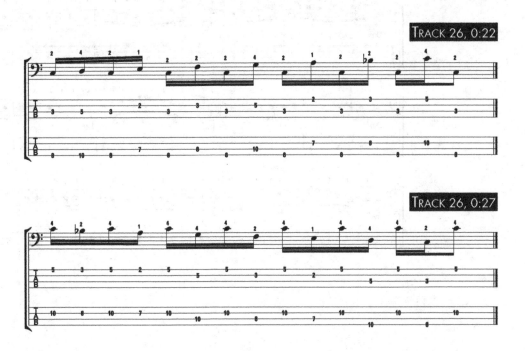

TRACK 26, 0:27

Notice that you can start these scales on either the E or A string, making this exercise ideal for playing grooves.

Rockin' Out

And now it's your turn to put all these exercises to good use. The song in the following figure is in a progressive rock style and utilizes sequences and grooves found in the exercises in this chapter. Make sure you follow the fingering indicated in the music so that you don't have to shift your left hand unnecessarily. It's very common for the bass player to play unison or harmonized sequences with the guitarist in this style and then immediately slip into a groove pattern without missing a beat (pun intended).

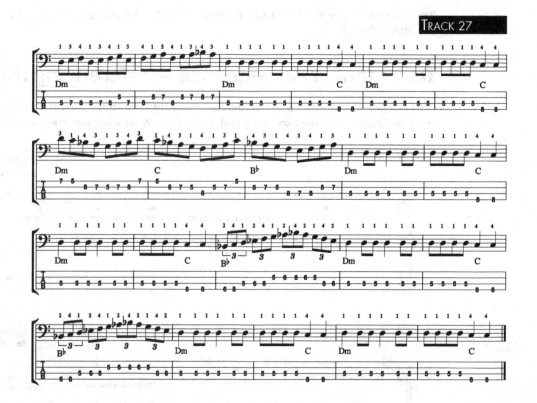

Chapter 5

Working with Arpeggios

Triads are the basic note structure in harmony. A *triad* consists of three notes — the root, third, and fifth of any chord. When playing a triad, you convey whether the chord is major, minor, or diminished, but not much else. Yet you can cover a lot of range on the fretboard via triads; they serve to get you from a low note to the next octave quickly and smoothly.

Playing triads as *arpeggios* (notes in a chord played one at a time) is an age-old way to develop musical prowess. You hear everyone from accordion players to jazz pianists, from classical to pop and beyond, practicing triad arpeggios to enhance their technique as well as their ear.

Triads: Outlining the Harmony

When you practice triads, you usually add the octave root at the end of the triad sequence. In the following exercises, you get to work on your "triad-athon" skills by playing arpeggios. You first get a firm grasp on the consistent pattern of each type of triad, and then you apply each in a musical setting.

Major arpeggios

The *major triad* forms the minimal outline of a major tonality and is embedded in no less than three different modes: the Ionian, the Lydian, and the Mixolydian (see Chapter 3 for more on these modes).

Start this arpeggio using your middle finger, and make sure you have a total of three strings to complete the arpeggio. Take a look at the grid and the music in the following figure.

Major

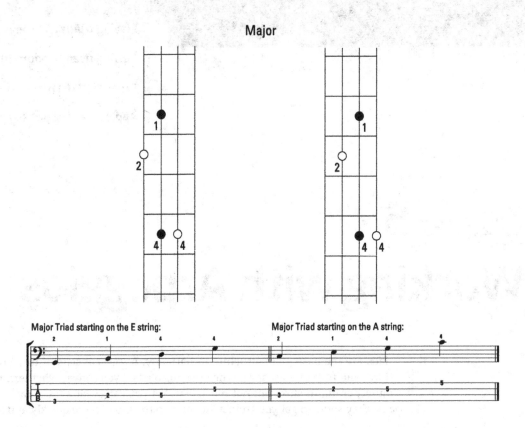

After you're completely sure-fingered, move on to the exercise in the next figure, which leads you through all 12 keys. Keep your fingering consistent throughout when you shift to the next position for each new arpeggio. Play the exercise in triplet rhythm so that it resolves rhythmically.

REMEMBER

You don't have to limit your arpeggios to the positions indicated in this exercise. Go ahead and explore the range of your bass. Just make sure you always start on the E or A string with your middle finger.

Minor arpeggios

The *minor triad* forms the outline of the minor harmony and is part of the Dorian, Phrygian, and Aeolian modes. The difference between the major and minor triad is only one note, the third, but it makes for a completely new hand position — and sound.

Take a look at the grid and the music in the following figure. You can see that you play the minor arpeggio starting on the E or A string, with your index finger on the root.

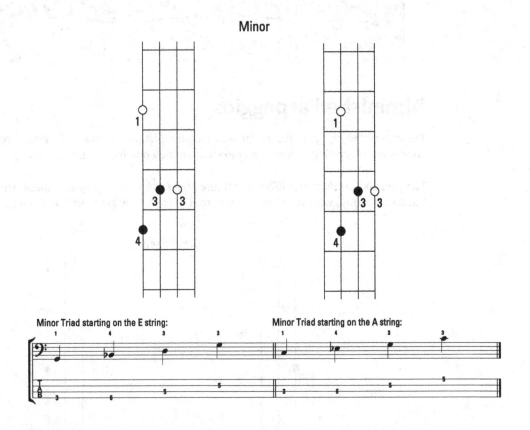

Practice the triad in the designated positions first, and then make sure to move it into other areas of your fingerboard. If you keep the fingering consistent you can play it anywhere without any difficulty.

When you feel comfortable with the fingering, continue on to the exercise in the next figure, in which you play the minor triad arpeggio in all 12 keys. Feel free to move past the indicated positions; just keep the fingering consistent.

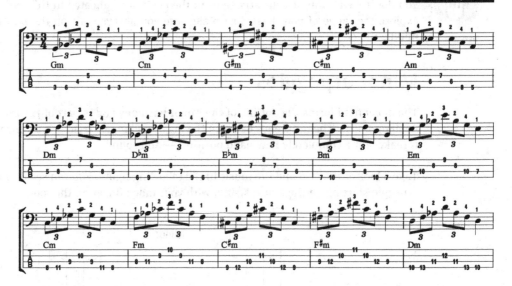

Diminished arpeggios

The *diminished arpeggio* occurs far less frequently than its major or minor counterpart, but it creates an interesting sound. It's embedded in only one mode, the Locrian.

The grid and music in the following figure show you how to play the minor arpeggio starting on the E or A string, with your index finger on the root. Now get your hands dirty!

Diminished

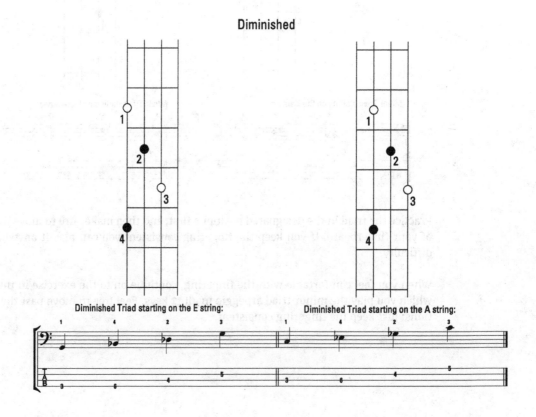

Work the diminished arpeggio as written initially, but then expand by starting on other frets. Just make sure that your fingering is consistent and that you start on the E or A string.

When you can play this arpeggio solidly, move on to play it in all keys, as shown in the following figure.

TRACK 28, 0:34

You're not limited to the positions shown in the exercise. They just help you cover all the keys. Feel free to play any of these exercises in other positions as well.

Getting Down with Chord Inversions

Inverting a chord means to put one of the chord tones other than the root on the bottom. In other words, if you play a regular C major arpeggio starting on the root (C, E, G), you may choose to play the same chord inverted, starting it on the third (E, G, C) or the fifth (G, C, E) of the chord. It's the same chord but with a different note in the bass.

You use inversions to make a chord sound interesting and unexpected, or to help you move smoothly through a chord progression. Either way, it's a good idea to have inversions solidly under your fingers . . . and in your ears.

REMEMBER

You can invert a chord whenever the spirit moves you, but sometimes you find a chord inversion specifically indicated in a musical chart. Inversions are written as two letters with a diagonal slash between them. The top letter represents the chord; the bottom letter represents the bass note.

Major chord inversions

In the following exercise you get to play the triad in root position, then play it with the third of the chord in the bass, and finally play it with the fifth in the bass. At the end of each phrase you restate the bass note along with the root to get your ear used to the sound.

When playing an inversion, always keep track of the chord's root.

REMEMBER The following figure leads you through the entire range of your bass — all keys and every fret, even the very top ones. You may have some challenges in reaching the top frets of your bass at first, but in time and with repetition, getting to them becomes much easier.

When you start in E or F, you need to use some open strings (not to worry, they're clearly marked). You play all the other keys with consistent fingering: You play all chords with the root in the bass using one pattern, all inversions with the third in the bass using another, and all inversions with the fifth in the bass using yet another. Just make sure you follow the fingering.

(b)

Minor chord inversions

All the basic rules for playing major chord inversions apply to playing inversions of minor chords. Remember to keep track of the root; play it at the end of each phrase to reinforce the sound in your ear. You play an open string only in the key of E; other than that, it's all patterns. The next figure leads you through minor inversions in all keys and positions.

(a)

(b)

Shifting with Two-Octave Arpeggios

One of the great challenges of playing a bass guitar is getting out of position and into the second octave. The trick is to simply treat each shift as a move into another position. You can cover great distances by moving via two-octave major and minor arpeggios.

The following couple of exercises help you play through the entire range of a four-string bass guitar and get your hands accustomed to the precise small shifts necessary to complete each arpeggio.

Two-octave major arpeggios

TIP

When you shift from one position to the next while practicing two-octave major arpeggios, make sure you don't take your eyes off the index finger of your left hand. The shift is only a distance of two frets, which means your hand moves by two frets. The notes, however, are *four* frets apart, but by aiming the shift with the *index finger* and then pressing the actual note with the *ring finger* for the major arpeggio, you only have to negotiate the relatively small distance of a two-fret shift.

Take a look at the grid for the two-octave arpeggio in the following figure. Pay close attention to which fingers are used for the notes. The pattern never changes. The only time you use an open string is when you play the E major arpeggio (you start it on the open E string). Make sure your shifts are precise and accurate. This is one of the great exercises that really gives you control of the entire range of your bass guitar.

Major

The next figure gives you the entire workout for two-octave major arpeggios. The shifts are the same throughout. Take your time getting used to the feeling in your hands — it's well worth it. You find yourself reaching the higher notes with much more surety after working on this for a while.

TRACK 31, 0:00

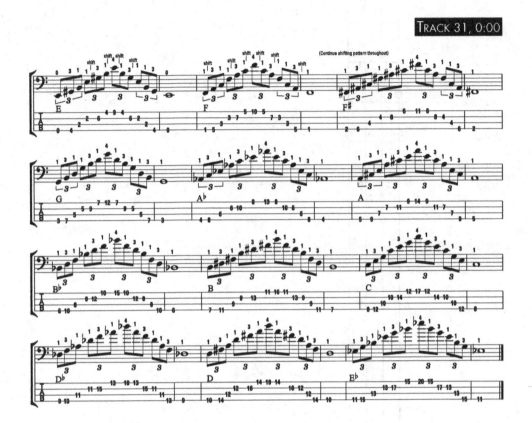

Two-octave minor arpeggios

The minor version of this two-octave arpeggio exercise is remarkably similar to the major. The shift still requires a move of the same distance — two frets if measured by the distance traveled by the index finger. The only difference is that after shifting, you press the note with your *middle finger* instead of your *ring finger*.

Check out the fingering grid for the two-octave minor arpeggio in the following figure and get used to the motion (and the sound).

Minor

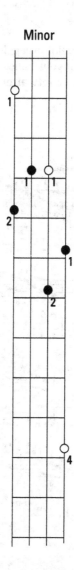

As with the major version, you use an open string only when playing in E. All the other keys follow exactly the same pattern, no matter where on the neck you play them. The shifts are indicated in the next figure for the first couple of measures. Follow this pattern for the rest of the exercise.

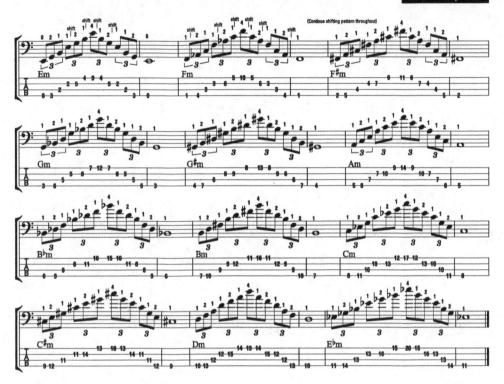

Using Triad Accompaniment in a Song

Triads are very popular in accompanying world beat tunes, such as reggae and African music. The structure of a triad contains enough information to tell the listener (and the musicians) whether a chord is major or minor but not enough information to limit the note choices of a singer or soloist. Try this next tune, and, if you find it sounds familiar, don't be surprised. This pattern has been used in countless songs.

Chapter **6**

Combining Seventh Chords

eventh chords are a hybrid between a triad (root, third, and fifth) and a mode (scale). Seventh chords consist of four notes: the triad plus the seventh note of the related mode. These chords run smoothly and easily through the harmony. Their sound signals exactly which harmony is being played, leaving no doubt as to whether you're in major, minor, dominant, or half-diminished (for more details on harmony, triads, and modes, check out *Bass Guitar For Dummies,* 2nd Edition).

Seventh chords in combination with modes are the backbone of bass grooves and solos. With just a few notes you can signal the harmony with perfect clarity. Modes are inextricably linked with their seventh chords; you have to be in full control of both to play satisfying and meaningful grooves.

Structuring Seventh Chords

You can play each of the main seventh chords — major, minor, dominant, and half-diminished — without shifting, as long as you have three strings to work with. Your bass has four strings (unless you play a five- or six-stringed bass), which means you start the seventh chords on either the E or A string to complete them without shifting.

The best way to get comfortable with the structure of each of the chords is by playing repetitive exercises throughout the range of your bass. These are the same chords you hear played on guitar and keyboard instruments; on those instruments, each chord is played as a stack of notes, all at once. Bass players integrate the notes of a chord, one at a time, into a groove.

Major seventh arpeggios

A true major seventh chord is actually less common in modern music than you may think. You do encounter one occasionally, perhaps in a very syrupy ballad, but most of the time you groove on a dominant chord. The major pattern does occur frequently in a melody line, however, so you don't want to be caught unprepared when a major seventh shows up. Get ready.

You start the major seventh arpeggio with your middle finger. Make sure you have three strings including your starting point to complete it. Check out the grid and the music in the following figure.

Major

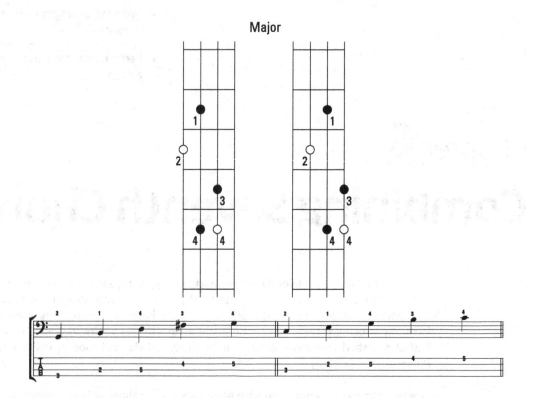

When you're on solid ground with the fingering and sound of the major seventh chord, starting on either the E or A string, take a stab at the exercise in the next figure, which gets you through all 12 keys and then some. Keep your fingering consistent throughout by shifting cleanly to the next position for each new arpeggio. Play the exercise using sixteenth notes to resolve it rhythmically.

TRACK 33, 0:00

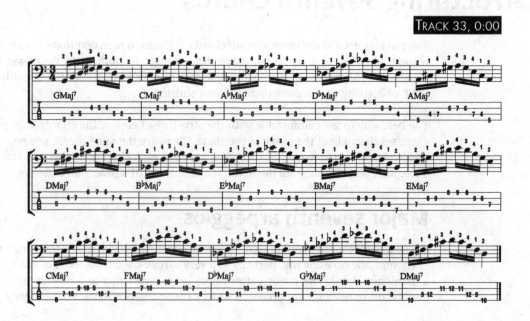

Don't limit your arpeggios to the positions in this exercise. Explore the range of your bass, making sure you always start on the E or A string with your middle finger.

Minor seventh arpeggios

The minor seventh chord is a very common tonality in a groove. You could say it's a great place to hang, at least musically.

Take a look at the grid and the music with the fingering in the following figure, and you see that you can play the minor arpeggio starting on the E or A string with the index finger on the root.

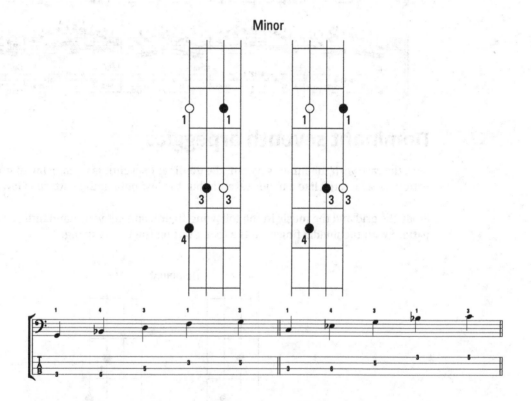

Minor

Play this pattern as shown, and then make sure you move the arpeggio to other frets as well. Keep the fingering consistent as you roam along your fingerboard.

When you're comfortable with the fingering, continue to the next figure and exercise your hands by playing the minor seventh arpeggio in all 12 keys. Move the pattern around on your fretboard and keep the fingering consistent.

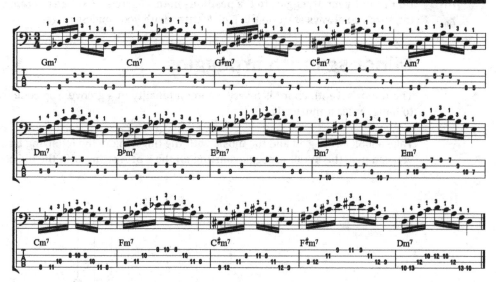

Dominant seventh arpeggios

As is the case with the minor seventh, the dominant seventh is a mainstay of groove playing. Its pattern is structured like a major seventh, but the last note in the pattern is lowered by one fret.

Study the grid and the music in the following figure, and get your hand into position to start this pattern with the middle finger on the root. Start on the E or A string.

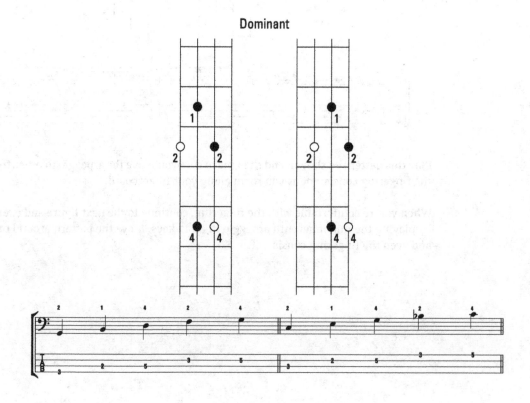

After getting used to playing this pattern as shown, make sure to move it to other frets as well. Keep the fingering consistent.

Continue to the next figure for a workout on the dominant seventh arpeggio in all keys. Move the pattern around and keep the fingering consistent.

TRACK 33, 0:51

Half-diminished arpeggios

The half-diminished arpeggio is even less frequently used than its major counterpart in a groove, but it shows up often as a short melodic pattern. Played alone, the harmony sounds almost eerie.

TECHNICAL STUFF

A note about the half-diminished: It's called a *half-diminished* because you lower only the fifth of a minor chord and leave all the other notes intact. (In a *full diminished* chord, on the other hand, the seventh is lowered twice and sounds like a sixth, or the seventh isn't used at all.)

Study the grid and the music in the following figure. The pattern is reminiscent of a minor chord, but with the fifth (the third note in the sequence) lowered by a fret.

Half-Diminished

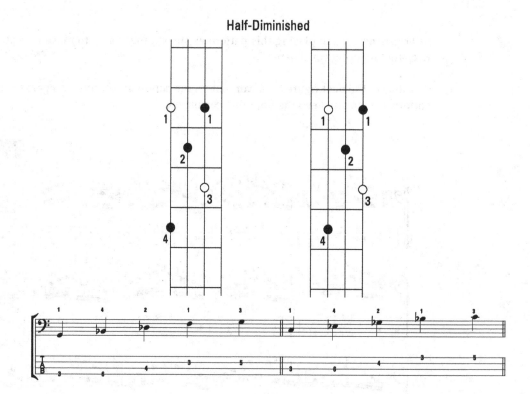

Get your hands used to the shape by playing it as written, and then expand it by playing the half-diminished arpeggio starting on other frets. Make sure your fingering is consistent and that you start on the E or A string with the index finger.

When you can play this pattern fluently, take it to all keys, as shown in the next figure.

TRACK 33, 1:16

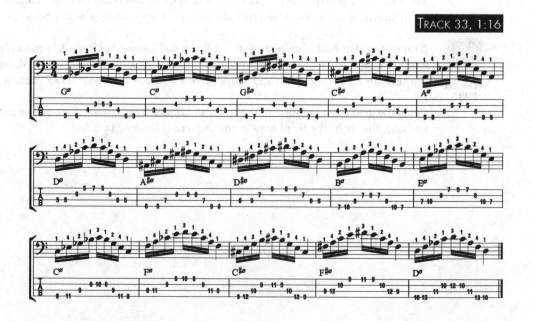

Don't limit yourself to the positions shown in the exercise. Feel free to play any of these exercises in any other position as well.

Combining Seventh Chords and Modes

If you remove every other note in a mode you get a seventh chord. By the same token, if you add a note between each note of a seventh chord, you get a mode. Modes and seventh chords are inextricably linked, especially for bass players.

In a great bass groove you find notes from both the seventh chord and the mode. The bass line usually weaves in and out, between chord and mode, to keep the groove moving and interesting. These next few exercises are great for getting used to applying seventh chords and modes to grooves.

Major seventh tonality

When listening to a piece of music, notice that the modes and chords don't just go up and down — they weave through the harmony. You want to play the seventh chords and their corresponding mode flawlessly so that you can extract notes from their regular up-and-down order to create an interesting bass groove.

The exercise in the following figure leads you through a major seventh arpeggio, followed by an Ionian mode (for more on modes see Chapter 3), and then a weaving of all the notes, out of traditional sequence. Finally, the exercise resolves to the root in the last measure.

TIP

This figure shows how to play the exercise only in C or G, but by consistently following the fingering you can transfer this pattern anywhere on your fingerboard.

TRACK 34

Major seventh groove, chord, and mode

To create the most lifelike application of the seventh chord and mode into a groove, I composed the special exercise in the next figure. The groove is a typical R & B-flavored pattern and is extremely useful.

This exercise sequence is lengthy and thus is shown only in two keys (to demonstrate the pattern starting on the E as well as the A string). You can move it into any key by starting it on a different fret and following the same fingering.

Minor seventh tonality

The minor version of the weaving exercise starts with the index finger, and it feels quite different from the major version. Its primary focus is on combining the seventh-chord arpeggio with the mode and then weaving through the notes. You use an Aeolian mode for this particular sequence, so you don't need to shift with this pattern.

In the following figure you get to play a minor seventh arpeggio followed by an Aeolian mode, and then you weave through all the notes in a crisscross pattern across the strings. The exercise resolves rhythmically and harmonically on the root in the last measure.

This exercise is shown in C and G. Starting on either the A or E string, feel free to use the same fingering beginning on other frets to cover the other keys.

Minor seventh groove, chord, and mode

The next figure shows you the most common use of this combination by incorporating the minor seventh arpeggio and its mode with an R & B groove in minor. The groove can be applied in many playing situations that require a minor harmony.

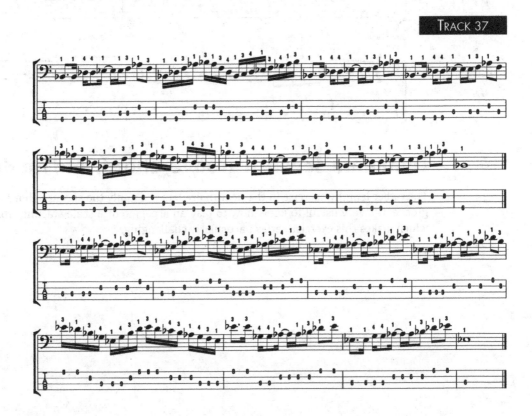

After you can play the exercise comfortably as written, go ahead and move it to other areas of your fingerboard.

Dominant seventh tonality

Dominant is, along with minor, the most common chord played in grooves. Note how similar this exercise is to the major version; only the seventh is lowered. Make sure you keep your hand in one position while playing this pattern.

In the following figure you play a dominant seventh arpeggio followed by a Mixolydian mode, and then you weave a line using notes from both. The weaving helps you stay within the pattern, even when you're not playing the notes in a traditional ascending or descending sequence. This exercise finishes on the downbeat of the last measure.

After you know this exercise cold and your playing is hot, move it to other frets, starting on the E or A string.

Dominant seventh groove, chord, and mode

The rather lengthy exercise in the next figure lets you apply the seventh chord and its mode to a groove. It's very useful to know how to play an arpeggio or a scale starting from the top down, which makes this exercise series particularly challenging.

When you can play this exercise solidly, move it to other areas of your bass. Go for it — you know you want to!

Half-diminished tonality

It's a very rare occasion indeed when you have an extended groove on a half-diminished tonality, but every now and then (especially at Halloween), you do encounter it. You don't want to breeze through major, minor, and dominant, only to falter on half-diminished and fully diminish your standing with your peers.

You can get comfortable with the half-diminished arpeggio, the Locrian mode, and the weaving of the notes in that harmony by sharpening your skills with the following figure. Stay in position and get used to the unusual sound of the harmony.

It may be half-diminished, but it wants to be played over the full range. You know what to do.

Starting on the
A String:

Starting on the
E String:

Half-diminished groove, chord, and mode

The next figure shows you the groove, arpeggio, and mode for the half-diminished tonality. It feels and sounds mighty strange, but only because you're not used to it, yet. In any case, it's a great workout.

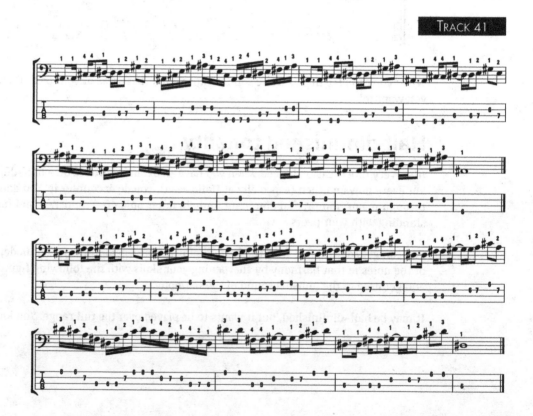

When you can comfortably play the exercise in the positions shown, go ahead and move all over the fingerboard. Keep your left hand in position . . . and don't keep making faces (I know it sounds strange).

Using Seventh Chords in a Song

Seventh-chord grooves are frequently played in songs that have long sections in a single harmony, usually minor or dominant. When you play a groove for such a section, it's up to you as the bass player to make it interesting. Keep in mind that you play only one harmony, using only one note at a time, so you have to do some good weaving to make it interesting. Enjoy playing the funky little song in the next figure, and make a weaver proud.

TRACK 42

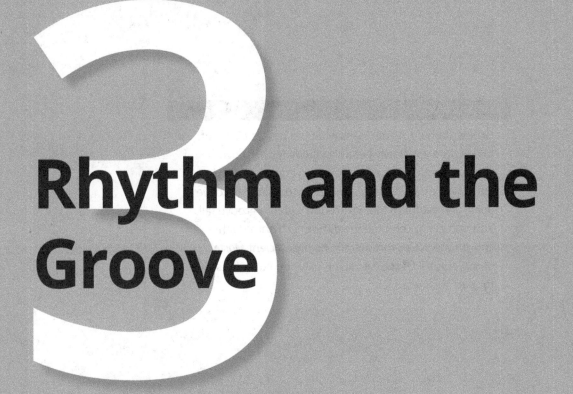

3
Rhythm and the Groove

Groove, baby, groove! That's what the bass is all about. In this part, you finally get a real guide for a groove workout that covers all the common genres and styles. You get to establish the groove skeleton, hit the groove apex, and establish the next round with the groove tail. You also get to combine the different rhythms with chords and scales through the highly efficient *Master Maker* etudes. Of course, all this is topped off with songs for each groove style.

Chapter **7**

Building the Groove Skeleton

G rooves are the bread and butter of bass players. The bass groove is the backbone of just about any contemporary popular song. It signals the song's tonal center, genre, tempo, and general feel.

The groove consists of three main elements: the groove skeleton, the groove apex, and the groove tail. The *groove skeleton* (the first two notes) is by far the most important element of them all, setting the mood for the entire piece. Some grooves even consist of the groove skeleton alone. In this chapter I show you how to keep the music interesting for yourself and everyone around you.

Playing with Eighth Notes

Each groove skeleton defines a specific feel and genre. You usually use the eighth-note groove skeleton in a rock or pop genre, but you can also funk it up by following the eighth-note groove skeleton with a sixteenth note or two.

Three types of groove skeleton use the *eighth-note subdivision:* the dotted quarter-note followed by an eighth, two quarter notes, and two eighth notes. The harmonic structure is almost identical in each of the grooves in this exercise series, requiring only minimal alterations for each groove sequence.

The first measure of each exercise consists of the groove skeleton alone; the next is a groove in a *blending pattern* that reaches below the original root (used when you don't want to attract attention to yourself), followed by a *bold pattern* rising above the original root (used to make a strong statement), and finishing up in the last measure with a syncopated complex pattern. Notice that you can play all these very different patterns using the same groove skeleton.

The following exercise warms up your ears as well as your hands to the sound of the eighth-note subdivision.

Dotted quarter followed by an eighth

A dotted quarter followed by an eighth note is one of the most commonly used grooves by bass players. You can hear it on countless pop songs, country hits, folk tunes, and whatnot. Just listen to Sting's "Fields of Gold" and the Beatles' "Ticket to Ride."

This exercise is a real-life experience of *working* a groove, not just playing it. You start out by just playing the groove skeleton. Then you add notes to it that are *below*, which creates a blending groove. After that, you notch it up to a bold groove by adding notes *above* the original root. Finally, you add more notes and *syncopated* rhythms (rhythms that don't fall where you expect them to) to create a complex groove.

All these grooves are very useful, and I urge you to practice them in different keys. The notes are ambiguous, meaning they can fit over a minor chord as well as a dominant, your most commonly used tonalities (the blending groove can fit over the major chord as well). Check out the notation in this exercise and get a grip on the grid.

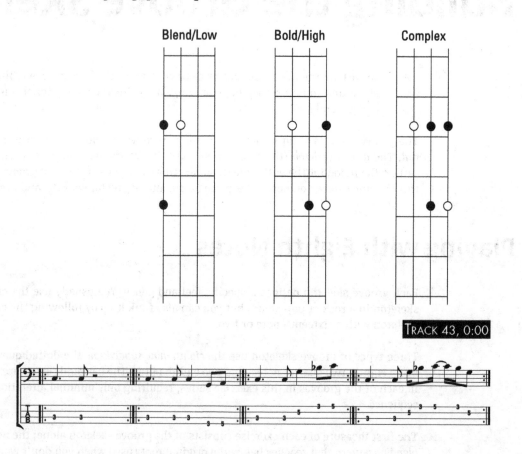

Blend/Low   Bold/High   Complex

TRACK 43, 0:00

Quarter notes

A groove that uses two quarter notes as a groove skeleton sounds more rock than pop. It gives you a very clear indication of the tempo and feel of the tune and is more "in the pocket" than the dotted quarter.

For easy comparison, all the grooves in this exercise series use pretty much the same harmonic structure. I'd call it *dominor* (a combination of dominant and minor . . . do we have a new term here?). Just check out the grid in conjunction with the notation in this exercise and enjoy playing it.

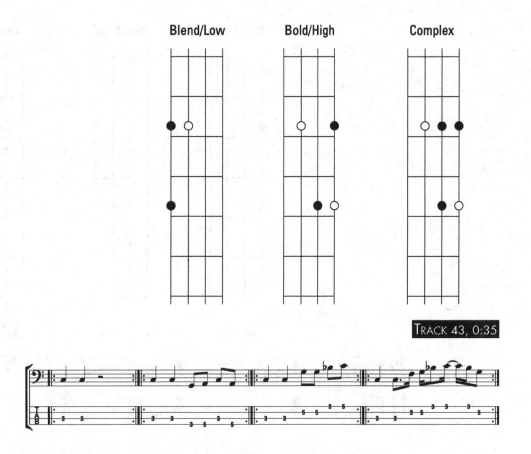

Play this pattern as shown, and then make sure you move the groove to other frets as well. Keep the fingering consistent as you roam along your fingerboard.

Eighth notes

You can use the eighth-note groove skeleton for driving rock songs as well as for some funk grooves, depending on the notes you use following the groove skeleton. If you follow with a simple eighth-note pattern (as in the blending version of this groove), it's rock; with a syncopated sixteenth-note pattern (as in the complex version), it's funky.

This grid, once again, incorporates notes that are fairly neutral. (What did I say? *Dominor?* The term is growing on me.) The notes are in a position in which you don't have to shift your hand at all.

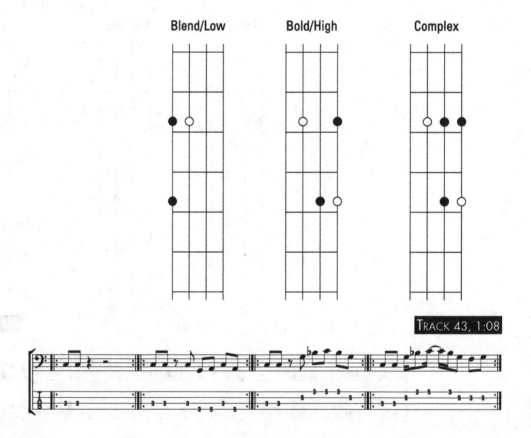

Rockin' out with a song

Move the groove patterns into other areas of your fingerboard. They're extremely useful — so useful, in fact, that you get to apply them in this hot little number, a rocker using an eighth-note groove skeleton.

TRACK 44

Zipping with Sixteenth Notes

Sixteenth notes are the funky part of the groove skeleton family. You usually employ them in accompanying funk tunes, or tunes that are supposed to have a funky flavor, like R & B and soul songs.

Sixteenth-note subdivisions include two main types of groove skeletons: the dotted eighth note followed by a sixteenth, or two sixteenth notes. You can create more variations, but they're rarely used.

As with the eighth-note version, you first play the groove skeleton alone, then in a blending pattern that dips below the original root. Next, you play it in a bold pattern soaring above the original root, and finally in a syncopated complex pattern, using the same groove skeleton for all the different patterns.

The following exercise warms you up with the sixteenth-note subdivision.

Dotted eighth followed by a sixteenth

Countless great grooves use this groove skeleton. It implies the sixteenth-note feel without the frenzy of starting the groove with sixteenth notes. Instead, you play a dotted eighth note and then follow it with a sixteenth to knock the feel into this complex rhythmic pattern. This groove skeleton makes for grooves that sound easy but are challenging to play cleanly.

Study the grid and the music in the following exercise. The patterns are once again harmonically ambiguous, so you can use them over a multitude of chords — minor, dominant, and even major — if you use the blending version.

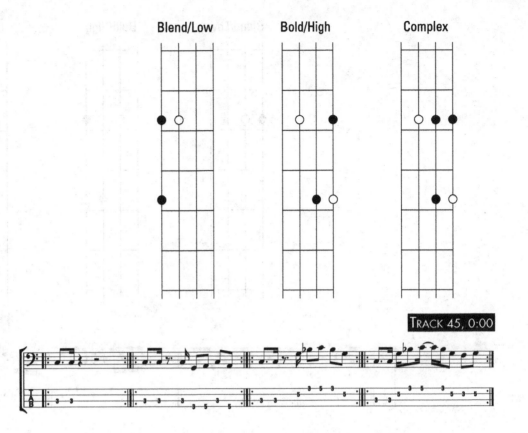

Get familiar — no, get very *comfortable* — with the rhythm and the grid of the grooves in this exercise, and then move them to different frets.

Sixteenth notes

REMEMBER

Starting a groove with two sixteenth notes is certainly the most aggressive and edgy way to lay down a funky groove, but keep in mind that the notes you *don't* play are just as important as the notes you do play. This holds true in any type of groove but is particularly important in a sixteenth-note groove.

The harmonic choice is once again a noncommittal ambiguous groove that fits beautifully over minor as well as dominant chords (okay, shall I coin it *minominant?*). Pay close attention to the space between the notes in this exercise.

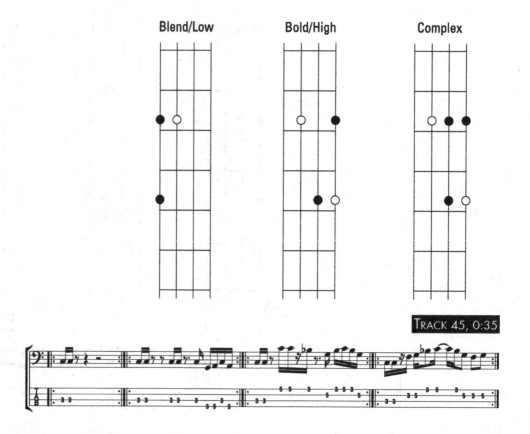

Getting all funked up

Now it's high time to get funky, so let that inner James Brown loose and get down with the number in the following figure, a song using a sixteenth-note groove skeleton.

Shuffling with Triplets

If sixteenth notes are the pushy, aggressive part of the groove skeleton family, triplets are their laid-back cousins. Triplets always give the groove a swing (or shuffle) feel, even if it's a bit funky.

The two most common groove skeletons in the triplet format use the first and third notes, or the first and second notes, of the triplet in beat one. Of course, the rest of the measure has to adhere to the triplet format as well. Get into the triplet mode by playing the notes in the following exercise.

First and third notes in a triplet

When you play the first and third notes of a triplet as a groove skeleton, you're playing the most common shuffle rhythm in the world. Thousands of blues tunes use it, along with countless other shuffle songs. The following exercise should sound very familiar to you.

TIP

Make sure not to let the notes ring for too long. This type of groove is often played on old bass strings — old as in, "They came with the bass, which I inherited from my great-granddad." You wouldn't have a lot of sustain on strings like that; to sound authentic, you want to simulate that sound.

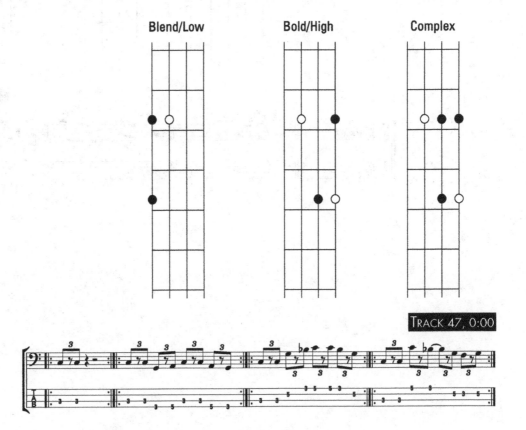

TRACK 47, 0:00

First and second notes in a triplet

Using the first two notes of the triplet in beat one as the groove skeleton gives you a very interesting, shuffle-funk feel. It's not as common as the previous shuffle feel, but it's highly effective when you get a solid grip on it.

This exercise gives you a nice workout for the groove skeleton, using the first two notes of a triplet, and it includes some very useful grooves, to boot. The harmonic structure is very flexible and doesn't commit you to either minor or dominant, which means you can use it for either. The extra note toward the end of the complex groove is simply a leading tone to the final note and not really part of the scale, but it serves the flow of the notes rather well.

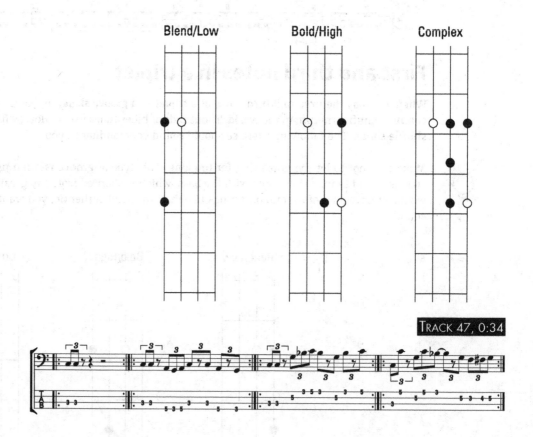

Trials, tribulations, and triplets

Triplet rhythm is right at home in the blues genre, and the blues genre is home to all kinds of trials and tribulations. Get in the mood for the blues with the following exercise using triplets.

TRACK 48

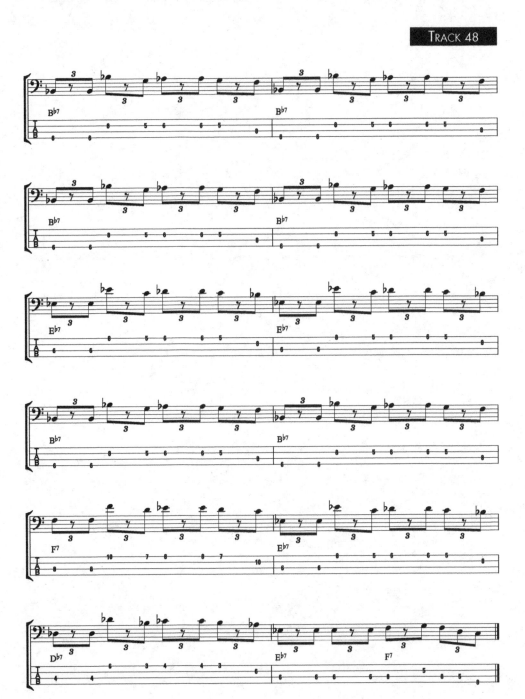

Chapter **8**

Accessing the Groove Apex

I magine that you're looking at a pond, and on that pond you see a row of ducks swimming. But wait! What's that? In the midst of the ducks, a turkey is flailing away, trying its best to stay afloat. Think you'd notice the turkey? You bet.

A *groove apex* is kind of like that turkey in the row of ducks. It sticks out, makes a statement, grabs your attention. The groove skeleton lays out the genre, tempo, style, and tonal center of a groove, whereas the groove apex gives it character.

You have to be in full control of all the subdivisions in each beat of a measure. You need to place a groove apex precisely, in order to create the greatest effect. This chapter shows you clearly how to plant the groove apex within each of the subdivisions and lets you hear how much it adds to the groove.

Isolating the Sixteenth Notes

A groove apex is quite often the note farthest removed *harmonically* from the root of the initial groove skeleton. It's what you hear as the high point of the groove. Determining which note is the groove apex is subjective — it's open to interpretation. The groove apex can be above or below the initial root.

In the following exercise series, you get to start with the same solid eighth-note groove skeleton and then practice placing the groove apex on each sixteenth of the remaining beats (on beats two, three, and four), using notes above and below the initial root.

You need to shift your hand when switching from playing the upper apex groove to the lower, but then you get to stay in position for each groove. The notes of the grooves for each exercise remain the same, except for the groove apex, so you can really hear and appreciate the difference that each makes.

Sixteenth-note groove apexes in beat two

You can place a groove apex in four different places in beat two: on the *two*, the *e* of two, the *and* of two, and the *a* of two. Each one gives the groove a different feel, and though some may sound familiar to you, others may sound exotic and are a challenge to play.

Listen to how a small sixteenth-note displacement can really give a groove fresh life. Make sure you play each apex exactly where it's notated — no fudging. The harmonic content is ambiguous and fits over dominant and minor (yes, it's a *dominor*). The first measure is an upper groove apex, meaning it rises above the initial root. It's followed in the next measure by a full-fledged groove incorporating the upper groove apex. The third measure includes a lower groove apex, which in turn is followed by a full groove using the same groove apex.

These grooves are very useful — the different groove apex exercises here help you solidify your mastery of all the subdivisions in each beat. This first figure helps you nail down all the possible apex choices for beat two.

Sixteenth-note groove apexes in beat three

As with beat two, in beat three you can play an upper or a lower groove apex in four different places, but notice the difference in the feel of each groove. The groove skeleton remains the same and so does the harmonic structure, but the groove fills in notes on beats two and four, leaving beat three solely for the groove apex.

In the following figure, you start with the upper groove apex and then continue with the lower, working your way through all the subdivisions in beat three.

Sixteenth-note groove apexes in beat four

The next figure covers all the possible places for a groove apex in beat four. This one can be tricky because the groove apex is getting very close to the downbeat of the next measure, so keep it nicely isolated. Beats two and three are now filled with notes, keeping beat four isolated for the groove apex.

Once again, you can place a groove apex in four different places within beat four — just keep a firm sixteenth-note count.

TRACK 49, 4:12

TRACK 49, 4:45

TRACK 49, 5:15

TRACK 49, 5:45

The rise and fall of the apex empire

It's time to apply the groove apex in a real piece of music. The following song is based on sixteenth notes, just like the previous exercises, and it's funky.

Isolating Triplets

When you're playing in a musical genre that utilizes triplets, you of course need to make sure your groove apex adheres to the rhythm of triplets. Thus, you can place a groove apex on three different parts of each beat: on the first note of a triplet, on the second, or on the third.

In the next exercise series, you start each groove with a groove skeleton on the first and third notes of the triplet in beat one, followed by the groove apex. Then you incorporate the groove apex into a full groove.

Your left hand stays in position for each groove so you can concentrate on getting the groove apex right.

Triplet groove apexes in beat two

In the following series, the groove apex is placed on the first, second, or third note of the triplet in beat two. Check out how the rhythmic feel drastically changes when you move the groove apex by one triplet note. The harmony of the groove is ambiguous, and you can find great use for these grooves, whether you're playing over a minor or a dominant chord.

As with the sixteenth-note version, the triplet groove apex exercise boasts an upper as well as a lower groove apex, and each one is followed by a real-life groove to demonstrate that particular apex. In this figure, make sure to get the triplets nice and even.

Triplet groove apexes in beat three

The next figure demonstrates the upper and lower groove apex on each of the triplet subdivisions in beat three. The groove skeleton is consistent, and the structure of the grooves is consistent throughout the exercise (with the apex moving, of course). Beats two and four are filled with notes, and beat three keeps the groove apex isolated.

Triplet groove apexes in beat four

The groove apexes on the triplets in beat four are depicted in the following exercise. Be very aware of how close they're getting to the next downbeat, and remember to keep them isolated. Just a short jab with the apex can give your groove a powerful effect.

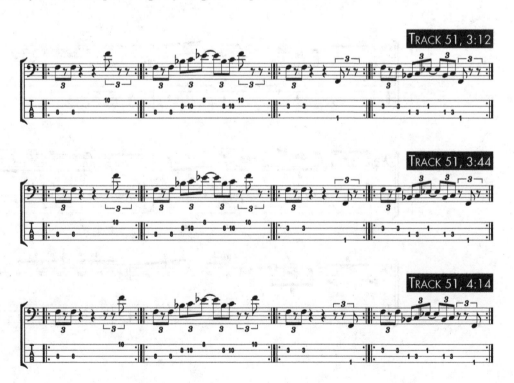

Having triplets

It just wouldn't do not to put the triplet groove apex to good use in a shuffle, which is, of course, a song type that uses triplets. In the following exercise, check out how the groove apexes are accented and really make it interesting for the listener.

Chapter **9**

Setting Up with the Groove Tail

Signaling to your fellow band members the beginning of each new groove, and what root you're approaching, is essential to keeping everyone on the same page — and in harmony. You accomplish this with the *groove tail*, or the back end of a groove; it's not just something that's tacked on without thought.

The groove tail occurs in the last beat of a measure and is your tool to get you to the beginning of the next groove smoothly and efficiently, leaving no doubt about where you're headed. A proper groove tail also helps you set up a new chord or a new section in a song. It's a signal to the musicians and listeners alike. This chapter provides you with some cool exercises to gain an understanding, and get control, of the groove tail. I'm sure by the end you'll be wagging your own tail with exuberant joy . . . if you have one.

Preparing a Groove with an Eighth-Note Feel

The kind of groove tail you use depends on several factors: the feel of the groove you're heading for, the number of notes you want to use to set up the next groove, and the harmony of the groove. The more notes you fit into the last beat of the groove (the usual place for the groove tail), the more urgency you create to get to the beginning of the next groove.

In all the exercises in this chapter, I use the same groove so you can compare the effect that each of the different groove tails has on the transition from the end of one groove to the beginning of the next. Check out the groove grid in the following figure, and bear in mind that this grid demonstrates the position of the notes for the basic groove used in all the exercises in this chapter; it doesn't include the notes in the groove tails. The groove tail changes with each new groove, and you need to follow the music and the tab for that.

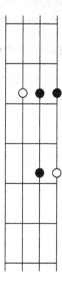

The exercises in the next four figures show great choices for groove tails in an eighth-note feel. The first exercise uses two notes for the groove tail, the next uses three notes, and the one after that uses four notes, followed by the final exercise using anticipations. The grooves all start with a groove skeleton that uses two eighth notes, and the harmony is a hybrid between dominant and minor, which means you can use it for either (*domin*ant plus mi*nor* equals *dominor*, which is pronounced *do*-mee-nor).

Two-note setup

The first selection of groove tails consists of two notes (see the notation in the following figure). You can hear how the notes move inexorably toward the downbeat of the next groove.

In the first two grooves, the groove tail approaches the next groove from below the root of the groove; the third groove's tail approaches from above the root. Both are excellent choices for a groove tail.

TRACK 53

Three-note setup

When you want to use three notes in your groove tail, you need to combine eighth and sixteenth notes. The notes you choose have to move with a common purpose and should all go in one direction, meaning they usually ascend or descend in a sequence. It's all about direction and flow.

In the next figure, the first two groove tails approach from below, and the third approaches from above. You want to get used to the sound and feel of each.

TRACK 54

Though this exercise is only shown in one key, you may want to play it in other positions on your fingerboard. Just keep the position of the notes consistent relative to one another.

Four-note setup

Using four notes in your groove tail means you have to use four sixteenth notes in the last beat of your groove — no rhythmic flexibility here. This is the busiest type of groove tail, and it definitely conveys a sense of urgency to get to the new groove (see the following figure).

REMEMBER

The trickiest part of a four-note groove tail is to keep your tempo consistent. Don't slow down when playing all those sixteenth notes in the groove tail, and don't speed up when you play the eighth notes of the next groove skeleton.

TRACK 55

Anticipatory setup

If you want to create the ultimate urgency in your groove, use your groove tail to anticipate the downbeat of the next measure, thus merging the groove tail with the groove skeleton of the next bar.

This technique requires complete control of the downbeat, so make sure you have a solid handle on the previous three exercises.

REMEMBER

An anticipatory approach lands you on your destination note (in this case, the root note that is expected on the downbeat of the next measure) *before* the downbeat. You play the note when it's *not* expected, and you don't play the note when it *is* expected. This technique gives the music a kick, like a roller coaster that suddenly drops toward the ground when you least expect it.

The following figure provides some great choices for anticipatory groove tails. When you play them with a drummer, it's a good idea to share your plans for an anticipatory groove tail so you can coordinate it together.

Tailing a song with an eighth-note feel

The next figure — a song using groove tails that lead to eighth-note groove skeletons — demonstrates how the groove tail sets up the next groove, even when it's in another tonality. The groove tail *always* adheres to the *next* groove; it always leads you to the next measure, the next downbeat, and the next harmony.

Approaching a Groove with a Sixteenth-Note Feel

The grooves in this section all have a sixteenth-note feel. A dotted eighth note followed by a sixteenth can only be subdivided with a sixteenth-note count — thus the term *sixteenth-note feel*.

The notes in the grooves in this section are all indicated on the grid in the first figure of this chapter. Notice that the rhythm is getting a bit busier. In a sixteenth-note feel you often have more notes per measure than in an eighth-note feel. The first three beats of each groove are identical (down to the dead note at the end of the phrase in beat three), so you can get the full experience of how the groove tail changes things up.

Two-note setup

To successfully transition from two eighth notes in this groove tail to the dotted eighth and sixteenth notes of the next groove skeleton, you want to subdivide your count for *both* into sixteenth notes. Keep the groove skeleton very tight — this is one of the more challenging rhythms.

The next figure provides an array of groove tail setups for your funky grooves. You can approach the next groove from above or below — just follow the examples and get used to each different sound.

TRACK 58

Get very comfortable with the rhythm and the grooves in this exercise and then move them to different frets.

Three-note setup

When you use three notes in your groove tail, you automatically combine eighth notes and sixteenth notes, which makes getting into the next sixteenth-note groove skeleton a little easier. The groove tail in the following figure approaches the new root from below as well as from above. It requires you to shift your hand out of position, so be sure to get right back into position for the next groove.

TRACK 59

Four-note setup

Setting up a groove with a sixteenth-note feel that uses only sixteenth notes makes perfect sense. You hit each of the sixteenth-note subdivisions in that last beat (your groove tail) and then fall right into the next sixteenth-note groove skeleton.

When practicing the exercise in the next figure, make sure you keep up the tempo with all those sixteenth notes flying around. Work out the fingering in the groove tail so you can get your hand smoothly back into groove position.

TRACK 60

Move the grooves with their groove tails all over your fingerboard. You never know where your next groove is going to show up!

Anticipatory setup

In the following figure you get to exercise your anticipatory groove tail . . . I guess you were anticipating that, right? The first two groove exercises anticipate the next groove by an eighth note; the third exercise anticipates the next groove by a sixteenth note.

Be very aware of where the downbeat is — you have no room for error.

A groove with a sixteenth-note feel that employs anticipation is the ultimate in playing an aggressively forward-moving groove. It's one of those grooves that seems to be getting faster and faster (without changing the tempo, of course).

Get some inspiration for anticipation and make sure to move it to other keys when you're ready.

TRACK 61

Song with funky tailing sixteenth-note feel

The next figure lets you connect different chords with different groove tails in a song format. Notice how the groove tails always aim toward the next groove. Listen to how each groove tail has its own personality, even though the grooves are all very similar.

TRACK 62

Setting Up a Groove with a Triplet Feel

When you're heading into a groove with a triplet feel, you want to set it up with . . . you guessed it, a triplet groove tail. A *triplet feel* separates each beat into three equal parts. The shuffle is home to the triplet feel, and you can find scores of blues tunes (and other styles) that use this feel.

The note choices are all the same for the exercises in this sequence, and you can find them on the grid in the first figure in this chapter. The groove tails give you quite a selection to choose from, and all of them lead to the next groove.

Two-note setup

The first two groove tails in the exercises in the following figure have an identical rhythm, which makes the setup fairly easy: Just stay in that rhythm. The third groove uses notes two and three of the last triplet to set up the next groove skeleton; set it up with a dead note on the first note of the triplet to give the line an easier flow.

You encounter a couple of dead notes in this groove. They help to move the bass line along smoothly without awkward silences. Just be sure to keep them thuddy.

TRACK 63

Three-note setup

When you want to use three notes for your groove skeleton, you need to play every note in the last triplet of the groove. This is a common approach for a shuffle groove and gives the line a nice flourish while setting up the next measure.

The groove tails take your hand out of position, but you want to make sure to shift back into position for the next groove. The triplets may take a bit of getting used to, but this is a great rhythm to groove on. Go ahead and exercise the grooves in the next figure.

TRACK 64

Anticipatory setup

And now for something completely new and fresh: an anticipatory groove tail in a triplet rhythm. Make sure you have a really good handle on triplets before attempting to anticipate the next downbeat, and subdivide every beat into three equal parts.

The triplet groove is generally more of a laid-back style of grooving (think the blues), but by anticipating the next downbeat you can give it the same urgency of a funk groove. Use the following figure for a good triplet workout.

TRACK 65

Happy tails for a song in a triplet feel

For a real-life application of the triplet groove tail, check out the next figure. Note how the groove tails all sound different, despite the similarity of the grooves.

REMEMBER

Always bear in mind that the sole purpose of the groove tail is to get you to the next groove.

TRACK 66

Chapter **10**

Combining Rhythms

G etting into a consistent rhythm and staying there — *playing* there — is pretty straight-forward. You count off to play in a sixteenth- or eighth-note feel, or a shuffle in a triplet feel, and at the end of the tune, you take a bow to roaring applause, never having left the sanctuary of that particular feel. However, at times you come across melodies or musical ideas that don't fit neatly into a row of sixteenth notes or a sequence of triplets. Sometimes the coolest melodic ideas combine triplets and eighth or sixteenth notes.

Playing two very different feels in one groove requires special skills. You need to be able to think of eighth- and sixteenth-note rhythms and triplets simultaneously and to switch from one to the other smoothly and effortlessly.

This chapter introduces you to some unusual exercises that help you gain a solid foundation in combining the different rhythms into the same musical sequence.

Mixing Triplets with Eighth and Sixteenth Notes

Mixing *triplets* (three equal parts of something, in this case of a beat) with *doublets* (two equal parts of something) is more common than you may think. You usually experience it in music that has a *swing* feel but is notated in a regular eighth-note feel. In a vast amount of music written in a straight eighth-note feel, you can hear an underlying swing in the bass groove — even in funk and rock.

Making your music swing means gaining control of both the triplet and doublet rhythm and also being comfortable with them together in the same phrase. The biggest challenge you face is switching instantly and making the transitions from one to the other as smooth as possible; these are skills that you develop only through practice.

The following figure is a warm-up exercise in which you get to play different subdivisions of doublets and triplets, moving from one to the other. The number of hits per beat (quarter note) gradually increases and then decreases, and you get used to the feel of each rhythm and its transition.

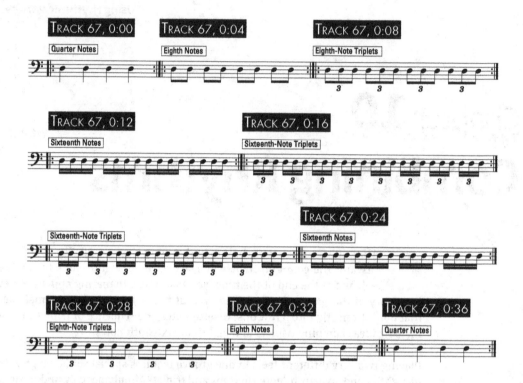

Scales in sixteenth notes and triplets

Scales are ideal for practicing sixteenth-note and triplet rhythms. Playing a scale from root to root (octave) provides you with eight notes. Playing these eight notes equally divided over the course of one measure means you're playing *eighth* notes. It also means you finish the scale before hitting the downbeat of the next measure, which is the most important beat for bass players — that's where you usually want to play the root note of a groove.

If instead you play four notes of the scale as sixteenth notes (one beat) and three as triplets (one beat), you can rhythmically resolve your scale by landing with the root on the next downbeat. The following figure shows you a great little workout using different combinations of triplets and sixteenth notes for major, minor, dominant, and half-diminished scales that all resolve rhythmically with the root on a downbeat.

Move these exercises to different positions on your fingerboard after you're comfortable with each of the scales' combinations. Just think of the convenience of practicing scales and rhythms at the same time.

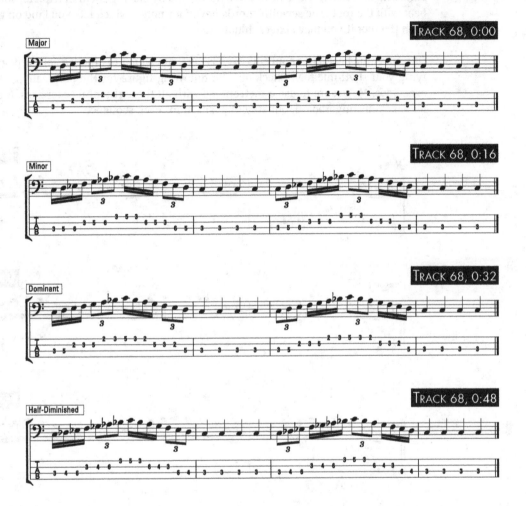

Arpeggios in sixteenth notes and triplets

Playing triad and seventh-chord arpeggios is perfect for practicing the switch from triplets to sixteenth notes. The triads have three notes, and by playing them in triplets, you land on the next beat with the root. The seventh chords have four notes, which lets you land on the following beat with the root if you play sixteenth notes.

Of course, the best part about this exercise is that you get to practice your arpeggios while solidifying your rhythmic feel. Check out the following figure for the politically rhythmically correct arpeggios. Make sure to use a metronome with all these rhythmic exercises. Move the arpeggios all over your fingerboard, but stay in position for each sequence.

Arpeggios and scales using sixteenth notes and triplets with a sixteenth-note groove

The ultimate in working with mixed rhythms is playing an exercise that combines triad and seventh-chord arpeggios, plus scales to rhythmically resolve into a groove. The example in the next figure does all this. Its groove has a sixteenth-note feel.

Your challenge is to play a smooth transition from the groove to the triplet rhythm, but you won't have much difficulty because the arpeggio in triplets is such a common sound. The scale goes past the octave root and on to the next note in the scale, the *ninth*. Observe the indicated shift and you can move through it easily. This example covers major, minor, and dominant scales.

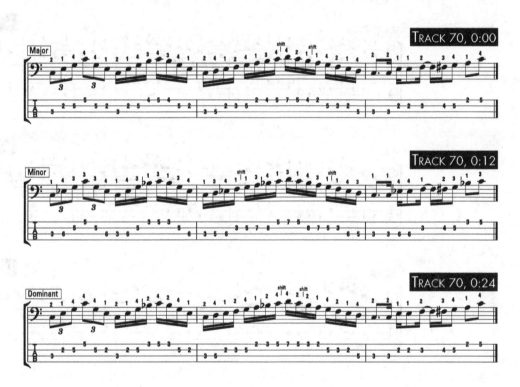

Arpeggios and scales using sixteenth notes and triplets with a triplet groove

When you divide the scale of the preceding exercise into triplets and sixteenth notes, you can slip easily into a triplet groove instead of a sixteenth-note groove. In addition, you save yourself a shift by playing the scale only up to the octave root.

Take a look at the following figure and note how similar this exercise is to the preceding one . . . until you get to the descending part of the scale and the groove. Note, too, that I use the Aeolian mode as the minor scale, so you don't have to shift at all.

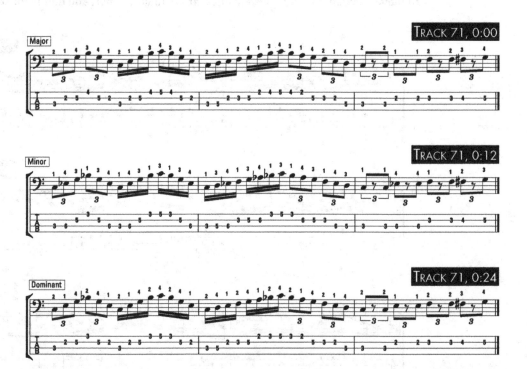

Song using triplets and eighths, with bass playing the melody

You're most likely to encounter a combination of triplets, eighths, and sixteenths when you play a melody on your bass. The famous song "Donna Lee" (recorded by the inimitable bassist Jaco Pastorius) is a great example of a melody that combines triplets and eighth notes. The following figure shows a song that requires you to go back and forth between triplets and eighth notes.

TRACK 72

Mastering the Master-Maker Etudes

A *master-maker etude* is an exercise that helps turn you into a master bass player. It's not exactly for the faint of heart. This type of exercise combines chords, scales, triplets, doublets, and movement over your entire fingerboard.

Bear in mind that after you master an exercise in one key, you can easily transfer it to another key by simply shifting to a new beginning note and keeping the pattern intact. This section includes a combination of exercises from previous sections in this book (arpeggios and scales); before long you'll be able to play the master-makers with ease.

Diatonic chord movement using eighth notes and triplets

The exercise in the next figure features a seventh-chord arpeggio in eighth notes followed by a triad in triplets, both moving diatonically through a major tonality. To accomplish this, you maneuver through several shifts, and by the end you will have traveled quite a range of your bass.

The overall meter of the exercise is 3/4, so your melodic sequences resolve properly. Practice the pattern first until you have it under your fingers. Then move on to work out the rhythmic transitions between the eighth notes and triplets.

Diatonic chord movement using sixteenth notes and triplets

The exercise in the following figure is a faster version of the preceding one, using sixteenth notes and triplets. The chord structure and harmonic sequence are the same.

With this rhythmic combination, you play in 4/4 meter. Remember to move this pattern (as well as the others) into different positions on your fingerboard so you can get comfortable with the entire range of your bass.

These exercises require quite a bit of string-crossing and shifting, giving your hands a good workout. Playing them is a great way to get yourself ready for some challenging music.

The ultimate exercise

For the ultimate master-maker exercise, take a shot at the tune in the following figure. It features eighth notes, eighth-note triplets, sixteenth notes, and sixteenth-note triplets, and it combines triads, seventh chords, scales, and a groove.

The sixteenth-note triplets are extremely effective if you want to play a flashy lick. You have six evenly spaced notes per beat when you play sixteenth-note triplets. You need to shift, in the minor version of this exercise, but not in the major or dominant. Enjoy this one — it sounds really cool.

Song with a rhythmically complex groove

Combining sixteenth notes with sixteenth-note triplets works best in a groove. Go ahead and apply all your newfound chops in the tune in the following figure.

TRACK 76

4
Turning Exercises into Music

Chapter **11**
Feeling the Eighth-Note Groove

G rooves come in three main categories: grooves with an eighth-note feel, those with a sixteenth-note feel, and those with a triplet feel. A groove's feel is defined by its groove *skeleton* — the first two notes you play in a groove. In playing a groove that has an eighth-note feel, you signal to the listener that you most likely are playing in rock style.

This chapter outlines which styles call for an eighth-note feel by the bassist (that's *you*). So, as they say, rock on, and in this case, don't make it too funky.

Harnessing Country Grooves

When you play bass in a country band, or even just play a country tune, you may think your job is simple, but that's not true. Country bass players may not play a lot of notes, and the note selection may be predictable, but they can speak volumes with those few notes.

Complete control of every note, including articulation and note duration, is the trademark of any good country bassist. Quite simply, precision is a necessity, because with so few notes to play you don't have anywhere to hide a bad one.

Traditional country bass

When you think of traditional country music, the names Johnny Cash, Patsy Cline, and Kenny Rogers come to mind. The song tells a story, and you don't hear the bass getting in the way of the melody. In fact, you'd probably notice the bass only if it were to drop out all of a sudden.

Traditional country bass lines usually consist of the root and the fifth of each chord, with an occasional walk leading to the next chord. The following figure shows notation and tab for the template of a typical bass line in this style.

TRACK 77, 0:00

When you play a country song, of course, you need to negotiate through more than one chord. Take a look at the chord progression in the next figure for some typical country music.

TRACK 77, 0:08

Contemporary country bass

Country music has become a fertile field of music, and many of its recent songs sound awfully close to rock or pop, getting more and more complex. In fact, the example in the following figure is what you'd expect the bass to play in a contemporary country groove. This line is replenished with dead notes, sixteenth notes, and even syncopation.

For a contemporary country song, try the bass groove shown in the next figure. Notice that you're still concentrating on playing the root of each chord, but your approach is much more rhythmic. As always in country, make sure to stay out of the way of the melody.

Caught between a Rock and a Hard Bass

As for noncountry music styles that require an eighth-note feel, two major categories stand out: pop and singer/songwriter styles, and the rock music genre. The pop and singer/songwriter format is a style you definitely want to familiarize yourself with. After all, pop is short for "popular." When you play in a pop format, keep this in mind: keep it simple, silly.

A pop tune is all about the melody and the lyrics, the stuff you can sing back when someone asks how that tune goes. (Only bass players sing back the bass line, and they're usually met with blank stares.)

Pop goes the bass player

Many of the early singer/songwriters didn't even use bass players for their performances, but these days they see, or rather hear, the valuable contributions a good bass player can add to their music. The following figure is your template for the bass groove in the pop and singer/songwriter styles. Note that you don't embellish your groove until the end of a long phrase, usually on the fourth bar.

TRACK 79, 0:00

A song in these styles may challenge you with a complex chord progression. As you play the exercise in the next figure, stick with the root, remember to lead with your fills only every fourth measure, and, per usual, stay out of the way of the vocals.

Rockin' and rollin'

Rock styles in music are unthinkable without a strong bass part. You usually concentrate on playing one specific groove pattern and move it from one chord to the next, adding plenty of embellishments every other measure, or thereabouts.

The following figure is a good example of a bass groove in rock style. Just don't forget to give it some attitude as you play.

TRACK 80, 0:00

In its purest form, rock consists of three chords, although many rock tunes have more. You can go through many a rock progression by playing the music in the next figure. Just don't forget that attitude!

TRACK 80, 0:14

Embracing Worldly Styles

World music refers to traditional music of a culture, usually played by indigenous musicians. As such, you can plainly see that this is a vast subject — as vast as the globe, in fact.

What really matters is that you're prepared to play a proper bass groove for any world music you're likely to encounter. With this in mind, I concentrate on presenting you with a workout that includes reggae, a couple of Latin styles, and a common African style.

These reggae and African styles may seem unusual choices to be lumped in with country, rock, and pop, but they're all part of the eighth-note groove family. So are numerous other *world beat* styles.

The harmonic structure of common world beat styles is usually pretty simple, but the rhythm is a whole new bass-ball game. You play rhythms that leave unusual spaces where you wouldn't expect them.

Ramping up reggae

The typical reggae bass groove is straightforward: root, fifth, with an occasional third and seventh, and with other scale tones thrown in as needed. In reggae you play the unexpected rhythm, leaving some downbeats open, after leading up to them.

You find many different reggae bass lines; the following figure gets you started with a typical example. Keep fills and embellishments sparse when playing this style, and make your sound dark and your notes short.

TRACK 81, 0:00

Reggae songs can have quite complex chord sequences, while the same rhythmic theme persists throughout. The next figure is an example of a reggae chord progression with a consistent rhythmic theme.

Looping Latin

Latin bass grooves come in two main varieties: on-the-beat and off-the-beat. Both are part of the eighth-note groove family. The on-the-beat variety is often flavored with a bit of a rock edge, as in some Santana songs.

Take a peek at the following figure for a common on-the-beat Latin bass line. Keep your fingering of the groove consistent; all the notes are within easy reach.

TRACK 82, 0:00

When you move a bass groove from chord to chord, be sure to retain your hand pattern throughout the chord changes so the groove feels familiar in every new position. Practice this by playing the on-the-beat chord progression in the following figure.

TRACK 82, 0:13

The next figure shows you an off-the-beat Latin bass groove. At first glance you may think that this groove is the easier line to play, compared to the previous example of an on-the-beat groove, but you may well find this to be the more difficult of the two. You want to keep the beat steady as a rock while avoiding playing beat one of each measure.

TRACK 83, 0:00

You need to anticipate the *next* chord when you're playing an off-the-beat Latin bass groove in a song. Check out the next figure and get into the groove.

TRACK 83, 0:09

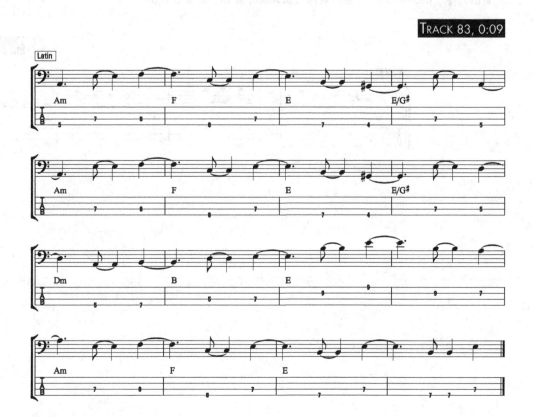

The whirled beat of world beat

World beat has as many styles as there are cultures, literally ranging from obscure individual African tribal celebrations to the German polka big bands (what a thought . . . a polka big band). The international grooves you're most likely to encounter are bound to have African flavors and are fusions of African and Western forms of music.

With this in mind, take a look at the exercise in the following figure. It's a world beat groove that's been around the world.

TRACK 84, 0:00

REMEMBER

The best way to approach playing a world beat bass groove is to form the triad of each chord and to use syncopation (you *can-can* find exercises for both in this book). The chord progression is usually simple and very repetitive, as in the next figure.

Chapter 12

Working the Sixteenth-Note Groove

You use sixteenth-note grooves when the music you're playing requires a bit of funk — a *good* funk, mind you. The main styles that lend themselves to sixteenth-note grooves are funk (of course!), R & B/soul (such as Motown and James Brown), metal, and prog rock (*progressive* rock).

REMEMBER

When you subdivide a measure into sixteen even parts using sixteenth notes, you not only have to play with great rhythmic accuracy, but you also have to choose each note very carefully. This chapter gives you a good idea of which notes typically work for the common sixteenth-note styles.

Getting into a Funk

Anytime you play a funk tune, the surest way to signal the funkiness, right from the start, is to put a sixteenth-note feel into your groove skeleton. The first two notes set the mood for the rest of your groove — you want it funky, right?

The two clearest choices for a groove skeleton in a funk style are two sixteenth notes or a dotted eighth followed by a sixteenth note. You can play in a funk style without starting with either of these rhythms, but starting with them makes your intentions undeniably clear — you intend to play the funky way.

Traditional funk bass

When you think of funk bass, you may think of the slap technique, in which you slap the strings with your right-hand thumb and pop them with your index finger, as Larry Graham and Flea do it. But bear in mind that funk can also be played using fingerstyle (Francis Rocco Prestia's style is a classic) or even with a pick (check out Bobby Vega).

REMEMBER

Funk is defined by rhythm, note choice, and attitude, not by any particular technique.

Traditional funk tunes stay on one chord or include only a very few. The groove itself is usually so busy that it provides enough musical motion to keep your ear (and your feet) occupied. Take a stab at the typical funk groove in the following figure, which shows notation and tab for a groove starting with two sixteenth notes.

TIP

Keep the notes short, sharp, and rhythmically precise (especially on the offbeats), and let the music get under your skin.

TRACK 85, 0:00

When you play a funk song, the chord changes are usually minimal, meaning that you stay on one chord at a time for long periods of time. However, the song usually has a "B" section that contrasts with the "A" section (see the song in the following figure).

Funk-a-di-gunk

Another way to play an immediately recognizable funk groove is to start with a dotted eighth note followed by a sixteenth. To get the feel for this, all you have to say is "funk-a-di-gunk" at a consistent speed. Your first note is on the "funk" (the dotted eighth), and your second note is on the "gunk" (the sixteenth). Try the exercise in the following figure for a very effective groove with this kind of groove skeleton.

TIP

Make sure to keep both starting notes sharp, precise, and consistent. Also, be very conscious of each space where you don't play any note. Space in funk is as solid as a brick.

TRACK 86, 0:00

As with almost every funk song, the chord changes are few and far between, with only a bridge section added for contrast. The following figure guides you through some static harmony.

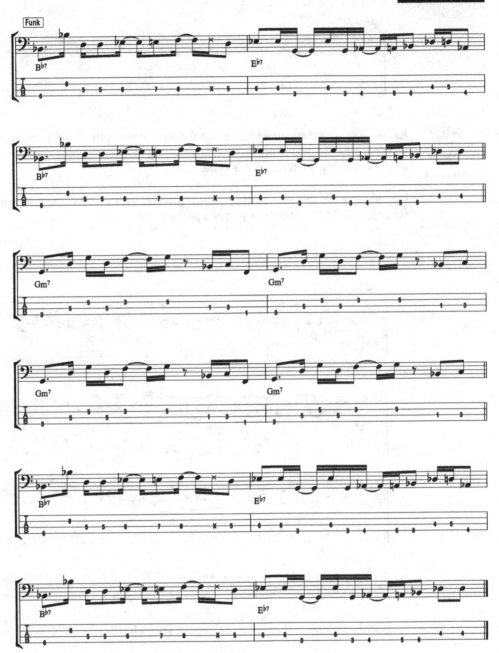

Funkifizing R & B/soul

R & B/soul is a genre that, these days, encompasses a variety of music. Generally, the songs are characterized by a funk rhythm but with a mellower attitude and more chord changes. The music is sort of like pop on steroids.

When you play an R & B/soul bass groove, you want to make it sound easy, even though you may well be sweating to keep all the notes going. It's busy without being overbearing. For a good example, check out the following figure, which uses a dotted-eighth and sixteenth note groove skeleton.

REMEMBER

As you play the syncopated grooves for R & B/soul tunes in all their syncopated glory, make sure you *anticipate* the next chord (arrive early). Doing so gives the music a strong forward momentum and is a defining attribute of this style.

Play along with the tune in the following figure and discover how a typical R & B/soul song sounds, at least from the bass player's perspective.

TRACK 87, 0:11

Be on Your Mettle with Metal . . . and Prog Rock

Within the *hard rock* family of musical styles you find metal and prog rock (*progressive* rock), both famous for their blistering sixteenth-note style. Despite the fact that both styles are part of the same subcategory, one is quite different from the other. The patterns in metal include repetitive notes: You strike the same note repeatedly before moving on. Prog rock, on the other hand, requires you to move through sophisticated harmony, often at breakneck tempo, and sometimes even to change meters in the process.

As you play these grooves, try to remember that it's not about the hair; it's about the fast and furious attitude . . . and sixteenth notes.

Steeling yourself for metal

Your role as the bassist in a metal band is to make the music heavy (as in *heavy metal*) and loud. You may want to reserve the loudness part for the big stage rather than your apartment, but you should mentally prepare yourself for some serious sonic onslaught.

Most important, you need the chops to keep up with the busy bass riffs. You can play with a pick or your fingers — whatever keeps you fast and steady. Make sure you have the stamina to keep up with the metal groove in the following figure for at least three to five minutes.

TRACK 88, 0:00

The songs in metal music are most often in a minor key, follow a minor progression, and quite often include some rather jagged harmonic twists, mixed with bass and guitar unison riffs. The next figure gives you a bit of insight into what a metal tune may sound like . . . oh, and watch the volume!

Progressing to prog rock

Prog rock can be a real bass slugfest. Sinuous bass lines that wind their way through complex chord progressions keep you on your toes as you negotiate fast passages and, occasionally, odd-meter measures.

Try playing the prog rock bass groove in the following figure slowly at first, as the string crossing is challenging. After you're comfortable with it, bring it up to tempo — that is, play it fast.

Most tunes give the bass player the freedom to create a bass line, as long as it's related to the tune's chords. In contrast, many of the prog rock tunes you encounter as a bass player are *through-composed*, meaning that your bass line is much more precisely defined and consistent. Needless to say, playing them requires plenty of rehearsals and practice. Take a look at the next figure for an example of what a prog rock bass part in a song looks (and sounds) like.

Chapter **13**

Trippin' on Triplets

When you think of triplet grooves, you probably think of good old blues — you know, sitting on the front stoop and lamenting your lot in life. Well, not so fast! Triplets are used for much more than just the blues, and it would behoove you to get a grip on this special rhythmic figure.

Triplet grooves are also commonly used for *shuffle, swunk* (funk grooves with a shuffle feel, as in *shuffle-funk*), and *hip-hop.* This chapter presents some cool choices you can try out the next time someone in your band doesn't want to play so square.

Shuffling the Eighth Notes

Anytime you hear one of those lopsided grooves just ambling along, chances are you're listening to an *eighth-note shuffle,* the most common of the triplet styles. If you have any aspirations of joining a blues or rockabilly band, this groove style must be in your bag of tricks.

The two most common forms of eighth-note triplet grooves are the *driving shuffle* and the *slow blues.* In the driving shuffle style, you play the first and third notes of the triplet during the first beat. In the slow blues style, you play one note on beat one and then initiate the triplet feel on the second beat.

Shifting into shuffle mode

You can play a very effective shuffle groove by simply striking the same note twice during each beat. In fact, that's the most common approach to the shuffle style. Feel is everything in a shuffle, so I advise you to spend some time getting a good rhythm going, even on just one note.

The way I notate eighth-note triplet grooves is just one of the methods you encounter in reading music. This method shows you most clearly the three subdivisions of each beat. Listen to the exercise in the following figure before playing it to get into a shuffle mood. You can hold the first note of each beat until you strike the next note. How you feel it is really up to you.

When you play an eighth-note shuffle, it's often a blues. The following figure shows notation and tab for a typical blues using the eighth-note shuffle groove. This song alone can get you through many, many hours of jamming.

The slinking shuffle

The slow blues is another common triplet-groove style, a sort of very slow shuffle. The feel is a bit different because you don't define the triplet rhythm until the second beat. You can also refer to this style as a *twelve-eight pattern* (four beats with three eighth notes in each beat).

REMEMBER

You want to have a really solid handle on your slow triplet feel for this style. The slow blues is far more difficult to play slowly while keeping a steady tempo than it is to play fast. Don't let the tempo slow down. It may sound (and feel) laid back, but it really keeps moving. Take a stab at the exercise in the following figure and settle into this feel.

The song you play in the next figure is yet another blues using a triplet groove. You often hear people refer to this style as *gutbucket blues* — a slow, usually sad rendition of a tough life. Please keep in mind that you don't have to actually *live* the life of a blues artist. Just read this book, listen to the audio tracks on the website, and *pretend*.

TRACK 91, 0:12

Swinging the Funk and Making It Swunk

At first you may think swing and funk are incompatible, but upon further examination you find that one of the hippest ways to funk things up is to swing it, using sixteenth-note triplets. This is also one of the densest styles you can play, with six subdivisions per beat instead of the four used in a regular sixteenth-note funk rhythm.

TIP

The sixteenth-note triplet funk, or *swunk*, is unique — completely unlike any traditional feel. You can find it in some modern jazz-funk tunes or in hip-hop beats. It's essential that you and the drummer feel the music the same way, as it's one of the more advanced grooves both of you can hook up with.

It don't mean a funk if it ain't got that swunk

By playing a funk with sixteenth-note triplets, you give the music a bit of a *swampy* sound. New Orleans funk is played with a swing. Jaco Pastorius's "Liberty City" is an example of this feel as well. It's very difficult to play and even more difficult to read.

Before you get into the swunk groove in the following figure, I highly recommend listening to the track on the website. Funk with a swing isn't something to read — it's something to *feel*.

The song in the next figure is an example of what a typical swunk tune looks like. You play the repetitive groove in the first section, feeling good, and then go on to the middle section, still feeling good.

Hipping and hopping

Generally, the bass grooves you encounter in hip-hop music have a triplet sixteenth-note feel. (Again, it's all about the feel.) Making electronic samples sound more human by adding your bass to the mix provides a wonderful opportunity for you to improve on the feel of machines.

TIP

When you take a peek at the groove in the following figure, bear in mind that hip-hop grooves are challenging to read. It's much better to listen to the recording first and then read the notation to see where you play the notes on your bass. Keep an eye on the 3 that signals a triplet. If you don't see a 3, play it as a regular eighth note.

TRACK 93, 0:00

In hip-hop tunes, you often find an overall sixteenth-note triplet groove in the main section of the song, followed by a section that features lots of space and sound effects, for contrast. The song in the next figure gets you hoppin' on the right foot.

TRACK 93, 0:10

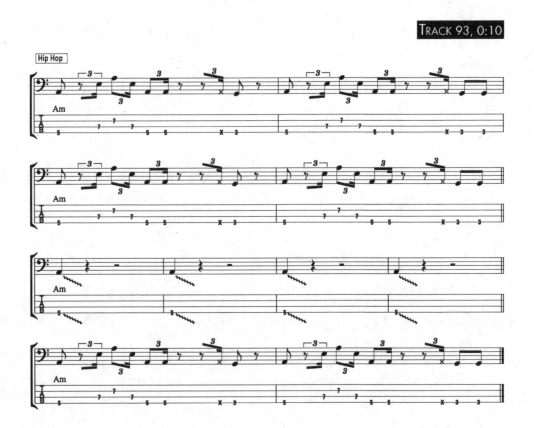

5

The Part of Tens

IN THIS PART . . .

Part 5 is the famed "Part of Tens" section, and no *Dummies* book leaves the press without it. Here you can discover why you practice what you practice. First, you get your very own practice regimen that will make you the ultimate bass player. You also get to see how other famous bass players have used the concepts in this book to create some magnificent music for bass. And now it's your turn.

Chapter **14**

Ten Essential Elements of a Great Practice Session

You may wonder how on earth you can possibly fit all the exercises in this book into your practice routine. It's simple — you can't, at least not all at once. The secret of an extremely effective practice session is that it covers all aspects of playing without wearing your hands (and your patience) to shreds.

Another important aspect of a great practice routine is that you design it with *you* in mind. You design your own, adding and subtracting exercises as you become a more skillful player. Quite simply, you keep rotating in and out of your practice routine exercises that essentially address the same aspect of playing.

Finally, the sequence of the different exercises is also crucial, and in this chapter I give you a fabulous template (based on more than 30 years of research, trial, and success) for your own routine. This sequence gets your workout into balance. You start with medium-to-difficult exercises, fill in difficult ones in the middle, and sprinkle in easy ones. That way you don't start out with just the easy exercises and run out of steam by the time you reach the hard ones.

TIP

You can keep track of whichever exercises you do by filling in the practice chart at the end of this chapter (I suggest you make a copy, or 20). So get ready . . . basses loaded . . . go!

Inverting Triad Arpeggios

Choose an exercise from Chapter 5. Just pick one of the figures; you can pick another the next time. Any of these will open not just your hands (given all the string crossings) but also your ears. Indicate the exercise and the tempo in the appropriate column in the practice chart.

Arpeggiating Seventh Chords

Now choose an exercise from Chapter 6. If you're really brave and you have the basic seventh-chord structures down cold, pick an exercise that also involves the scale, like one of the "weave" patterns later in that chapter. Enter the exercise in the practice chart, including the tempo you're playing, and move on.

Playing Scale Sequences with Grooves

Pick an exercise from Chapter 4. The scale sequence exercises, followed by a groove, are a definite step up in the difficulty factor. The results are simply fabulous (and sound pleasant, to boot). Note the exercise and tempo in your chart and go to the next element.

Moving the Modes

Choose an exercise from Chapter 3. You now get to take a bit of a breather by playing the modes in a linear fashion and thus embedding them into your memory banks. Write the mode and exercise into your chart, and don't forget to note the tempo.

Doing Right-Hand Exercises

Turn to Chapter 2 and select one of the exercises that emphasize your right hand. Your right hand (the striking hand) gets to work out while your fretting hand takes a breather. Really concentrate on the hand you're working. Log the exercise and tempo into your chart and move on to the next.

Doing Left-Hand Exercises

Turn to Chapter 2 and select one of the exercises that emphasize your left hand. Personally, I feel the best one is the left-hand permutation etude, but don't forget about the others. Mark the exercise into your practice chart with the appropriate tempo and go on.

Practicing Master-Maker Etudes

Choose an exercise in Chapter 10. Needless to say, the master-maker etudes are there to challenge you, so look at this as your grand finale in terms of the workout. You're now combining rhythms, scales, chords, and grooves in one very dense exercise. Write down which one you tackle and don't forget to note the tempo. Then move to the next.

Grooving in a Genre/Style

It's reward time. Choose a groove in a particular style from Chapter 11, 12, or 13. This part of the routine should be pleasant, so enjoy rocking out, exploring country, getting funky, or shuffling to your heart's content. Just make sure to keep track of which style you practice so you can rotate them all. Note the exercise in your chart and continue.

Freebassing

Huh? Yes, you read that correctly. At this point you simply play whatever comes to mind. It could be a solo, a groove, a song — whatever. The point is to have a period in your practice routine during which you can fully express yourself *without judgment or restrictions*. Some great stuff can come out of such "freebassing," so feel free to take notes on your practice sheet (mode, tonality, style, tempo) and move on.

Reading Bass Grooves

Finally, pick any of the songs or grooves from this book and practice reading the notation. You can use the tab as a crutch at first, but get used to looking at the notes and knowing what a certain phrase sounds like. Keep it short, especially at first, but do it often. After you master reading, you can get a lot of information from all kinds of books and sheet music.

Bass Practice Routine

Warm-up	Etude	Tempo
Arpeggio Inversions		
Seventh-Chord Arpeggios		
Scale Sequences with Grooves		
Modes		
Right-Hand Etudes		
Left-Hand Etudes		
Master-Maker Etudes		
Groove		
Free Bass		
Reading		

Chapter 15

Ten Famous Tunes That Incorporate the Exercises in This Book

Why do I tell you to do the exercises in this book? So you can become a better bass player? Increase your technical and musical ability? Of course, that's a big part of it, but there's more. You can use these exercises to play music, songs, and grooves.

The exercises in *Bass Guitar Exercises For Dummies* are based on real-life music. As you practice them, you're honing your skills to play songs. What better way to demonstrate this concept than by showing you examples of ten famous and successful tunes that incorporate exercises from this book as bass lines?

In this chapter you find a list of ten fabulous bass players playing ten unforgettable songs. Hear for yourself why you're putting in all the hard hours practicing the exercises I show you.

TIP

Unfortunately, copyright laws don't let me quote these songs in this book or copy them to the website, but I do provide you with a link to them from my Web site: www.sourkrautmusic.com.

From here you can discover, or rediscover, these bass gems and listen to them from a whole new perspective.

Weaving through Scales and Chords — Jaco Pastorius

Jaco Pastorius's performance on "Come On, Come Over" (from his self-titled album) is a stunning example of a groove that weaves through the tonality while leaving the fretting hand in position (see Chapter 6). When you listen to the recording, wait for the chorus (which comes about 56 seconds into the tune) to hear Jaco manhandling the groove, sprinkling it with some tasty dead notes (see Chapter 2) along the way.

Perfecting the Groove Tail — Pino Palladino

Paul Young's hit "Everytime You Go Away" contains a terrific example of groove tails (see Chapter 9), executed to perfection by bassist Pino Palladino. His bass part is an integral part of the song and is a beautiful example of how the bass can contribute mightily to a hit.

Inverting Triad Arpeggios — Cliff Burton

The song "Anesthesia (Pulling Teeth)" by the metal band Metallica is probably one of the most famous bass performances by the legendary Cliff Burton. This bass solo is constructed primarily of triads and their inversions (see Chapter 5) and is a classic.

Swinging the Triplets — Berry Oakley

Berry Oakley, bassist for the Allman Brothers Band, gives a perfect performance on the famous blues tune "Stormy Monday," playing a beautiful triplet rhythm in his groove (see Chapter 13). You can just feel each note oozing with the blues.

Hitting the Groove Apex — David Hood

The unforgettable hit "I'll Take You There" by the Staple Singers features an excellent example of how the groove apex (see Chapter 8) can take a song to a whole new level of perfection. David Hood's performance of this irresistible bass line is a classic that all bass players need to check out.

Arpeggiating the Triad — Paul McCartney

Perhaps the most famous of all bass players, Paul McCartney of the Beatles is the performer of a groove constructed of triads (see Chapter 5) straight up and down. The song is the well-known "Ob-La-Di, Ob-La-Da."

Nailing the Groove Skeleton — Anthony Jackson

Master bassist Anthony Jackson's performance of "For the Love of Money" by the O'Jays is a perfect example of a consistent groove skeleton (see Chapter 7) that drives a powerful groove and makes a song absolutely funky. This song thrives on the bass part.

Using the Seventh-Chord Arpeggio — George Porter, Jr.

George Porter, Jr., bass player for the famous New Orleans funk band the Meters, lays down one of the coolest examples of a seventh-chord arpeggio (see Chapter 6) in his groove for "Cissy Strut." The descending minor seventh arpeggio *is* the groove theme, and the song is representative of the special funk that's native to the Crescent City.

Running the Mode — Bernard Edwards

One of the giants of the disco era, the group Chic and its bass player Bernard Edwards landed a massive hit with "Good Times," in which Edwards builds the famous bass line on a simple Dorian mode (see Chapter 3). Who said playing scales has to be boring?

Mastering the Swunk — Francis "Rocco" Prestia

The West Coast–based horn band Tower of Power rightly has a stellar reputation for having one of the absolute funkiest rhythm sections on the planet. Anchored by bassist Francis "Rocco" Prestia, they display a fabulous swunk groove (see Chapter 13) on their tune "Pocketful of Soul." Pure ear candy.

6
Appendixes

Appendix A explains how to use the audio files on the website and lists all of its tracks. Appendix B provides a little extra info on extended-range basses and ends with a weekly practice goal sheet that you can copy and use to keep track of your progress as you become more proficient playing the bass.

Appendix A

How to Use the Website

You can hear almost every example of music in *Bass Guitar Exercises For Dummies* on the web page that corresponds to this book at www.dummies.com/go/bassguitarexercisesfd. The text in the book explains the different techniques and styles, the figures show you examples in music notation, and the web page demonstrates how the examples sound when played correctly.

TIP

Having the web page loaded and then playing the appropriate examples as you read about them in the text is a great way to experience this book in all its glory. When you hear an example that you just have to try, grab your bass and play it. If the example is beyond your grasp, go to an earlier section and work out your technique.

Note: If you're using a digital version of this book, go to www.dummies.com/go/bassguitarexercisesfd for access to the music tracks.

Relating the Text to the Website Files

Every musical example in this book has a small black bar (the track bar) that tells you where the example is located on the track list. The track bar gives you the track number and the start time (in minutes and seconds) for each example. You can then cue up the track on the web page to hear it.

If you're searching for an example within an audio track, use the cue button of the cue/review function (also known as the *fast forward/rewind* control) of the media player to go to the specific time, indicated in minutes and seconds, within that track. When you get on or near the start time, release the cue button and the example plays.

TIP

If you want to play along with the audio track, give yourself some extra time by cueing up a few seconds before the desired example starts (for example, in the case of Track 18, 0:33, you may want to cue up to Track 18, 0:28). Given the few extra seconds, you have time to toss the remote and get your bass into playing position before the music starts.

Stereo separation

All the songs feature bass, guitar, and drums and are recorded in what's known as *stereo split*; the bass is recorded on only one of the channels, the left. In the examples, you can hear the entire band if the *balance control* on your stereo is in its normal position (straight up). If you want to hear more of the bass, just turn the balance control to the left. If you feel that you can hang with the guitarist and drummer alone, just turn the balance control all the way to the right. You can then play to your heart's content with just you playing the bass parts.

Stereo split works on your computer as well. Just find your system preferences and go to the sound tab. In this tab, you should come across the output and be able to pan your stereo sound left or right. You need to have external speakers or headphones hooked up to your headphone jack.

System Requirements

Make sure your computer meets the minimum system requirements shown in the following list. If your computer doesn't match up to most of these requirements, you may have problems using the software and files on the website.

>> A PC running Microsoft Windows or Linux with kernel 2.4 or later or a Macintosh running Apple OS X or later

>> An Internet connection

>> A web browser

Tracks on the Web page

The following list shows the tracks on the Web page, along with the track times and chapter numbers that match up with them in the book.

Enjoy listening and playing along!

Track	Time	Chapter
1	0:00	Ch. 3
	0:11	Ch. 3
	0:23	Ch. 3
	0:45	Ch. 3
	0:56	Ch. 3
	1:07	Ch. 3
	1:30	Ch. 3
	1:42	Ch. 3
	1:54	Ch. 3
	2:17	Ch. 3
	2:29	Ch. 3
	2:40	Ch. 3
	3:03	Ch. 3
	3:15	Ch. 3
	3:27	Ch. 3
	3:50	Ch. 3

Track	Time	Chapter
	4:02	Ch. 3
	4:14	Ch. 3
	4:36	Ch. 3
	4:49	Ch. 3
	5:01	Ch. 3
2		Ch. 3
3	0:00	Ch. 4
	0:21	Ch. 4
4	0:00	Ch. 4
	0:09	Ch. 4
	0:19	Ch. 4
5		Ch. 4
6	0:00	Ch. 4
	0:09	Ch. 4
7		Ch. 4
8	0:00	Ch. 4
	0:21	Ch. 4
9	0:00	Ch. 4
	0:09	Ch. 4
	0:20	Ch. 4
10		Ch. 4
11		Ch. 4
12		Ch. 4
13		Ch. 4
14	0:00	Ch. 4
	0:06	Ch. 4
	0:13	Ch. 4
	0:20	Ch. 4
15		Ch. 4
16	0:00	Ch. 4
	0:06	Ch. 4
17		Ch. 4
18	0:00	Ch. 4
	0:06	Ch. 4

(continued)

(continued)

Track	Time	Chapter
19		Ch. 4
20	0:00	Ch. 4
	0:06	Ch. 4
	0:13	Ch. 4
	0:19	Ch. 4
21		Ch. 4
22	0:00	Ch. 4
	0:06	Ch. 4
23		Ch. 4
24	0:00	Ch. 4
	0:06	Ch. 4
25		Ch. 4
26	0:00	Ch. 4
	0:05	Ch. 4
	0:11	Ch. 4
	0:17	Ch. 4
	0:22	Ch. 4
	0:27	Ch. 4
27		Ch. 4
28	0:00	Ch. 5
	0:16	Ch. 5
	0:34	Ch. 5
29		Ch. 5
30		Ch. 5
31	0:00	Ch. 5
	0:27	Ch. 5
32		Ch. 5
33	0:00	Ch. 6
	0:24	Ch. 6
	0:51	Ch. 6
	1:16	Ch. 6
34		Ch. 6
35		Ch. 6

Track	Time	Chapter
36		Ch. 6
37		Ch. 6
38		Ch. 6
39		Ch. 6
40		Ch. 6
41		Ch. 6
42		Ch. 6
43	0:00	Ch. 7
	0:35	Ch. 7
	1:08	Ch. 7
44		Ch. 7
45	0:00	Ch. 7
	0:35	Ch. 7
46		Ch. 7
47	0:00	Ch. 7
	0:34	Ch. 7
48		Ch. 7
49	0:00	Ch. 8
	0:33	Ch. 8
	1:03	Ch. 8
	1:33	Ch. 8
	2:06	Ch. 8
	2:39	Ch. 8
	3:09	Ch. 8
	3:39	Ch. 8
	4:12	Ch. 8
	4:45	Ch. 8
	5:15	Ch. 8
	5:45	Ch. 8
50		Ch. 8
51	0:00	Ch. 8
	0:32	Ch. 8
	1:02	Ch. 8
	1:35	Ch. 8

(continued)

Track	Time	Chapter
	2:08	Ch. 8
	2:39	Ch. 8
	3:12	Ch. 8
	3:44	Ch. 8
	4:14	Ch. 8
52		Ch. 8
53		Ch. 9
54		Ch. 9
55		Ch. 9
56		Ch. 9
57		Ch. 9
58		Ch. 9
59		Ch. 9
60		Ch. 9
61		Ch. 9
62		Ch. 9
63		Ch. 9
64		Ch. 9
65		Ch. 9
66		Ch. 9
67	0:00	Ch. 10
	0:04	Ch. 10
	0:08	Ch. 10
	0:12	Ch. 10
	0:16	Ch. 10
	0:24	Ch. 10
	0:28	Ch. 10
	0:32	Ch. 10
	0:36	Ch. 10
68	0:00	Ch. 10
	0:16	Ch. 10
	0:32	Ch. 10
	0:48	Ch. 10
69	0:00	Ch. 10

Track	Time	Chapter
	0:12	Ch. 10
	0:24	Ch. 10
	0:36	Ch. 10
70	0:00	Ch. 10
	0:12	Ch. 10
	0:24	Ch. 10
71	0:00	Ch. 10
	0:12	Ch. 10
	0:24	
72		Ch. 10
73		Ch. 10
74		Ch. 10
75	0:00	Ch. 10
	0:15	Ch. 10
	0:31	Ch. 10
76		Ch. 10
77	0:00	Ch. 11
	0:08	Ch. 11
78	0:00	Ch. 11
	0:16	Ch. 11
79	0:00	Ch. 11
	0:17	Ch. 11
80	0:00	Ch. 11
	0:14	Ch. 11
81	0:00	Ch. 11
	0:14	Ch. 11
82	0:00	Ch. 11
	0:13	Ch. 11
83	0:00	Ch. 11
	0:09	Ch. 11
84	0:00	Ch. 11
	0:10	Ch. 11
85	0:00	Ch. 12
	0:08	Ch. 12

(continued)

(continued)

Track	Time	Chapter
86	0:00	Ch. 12
	0:14	Ch. 12
87	0:00	Ch. 12
	0:11	Ch. 12
88	0:00	Ch. 12
	0:08	Ch. 12
89	0:00	Ch. 12
	0:10	Ch. 12
90	0:00	Ch. 13
	0:07	Ch. 13
91	0:00	Ch. 13
	0:12	Ch. 13
92	0:00	Ch. 13
	0:12	Ch. 13
93	0:00	Ch. 13
	0:10	Ch. 13

Troubleshooting

If you have trouble with the website, please call Customer Service at 877-762-2974 (outside the U.S.: 317-572-3993) or send e-mail to techsupdum@wiley.com. Wiley Publishing, Inc., will provide technical support only for installation and other general quality-control items.

Appendix B

Extended Range Basses and Practice Goals

Throughout this book, I give you all kinds of exercises to elevate your bass playing, and all the exercises fall within the range of a four-string bass guitar. But alas, what are you to do if your particular bass exceeds the string count and sports one or even two additional strings? No worries! This appendix addresses the notation of so-called *extended range* basses by showing you not only the location of every single note on their fingerboard but also what each note looks like in regular music notation.

The following figures deal with five- and six-string basses and how the tab and the notation relate to the actual frets on the fingerboard. You can then play the exercises in this book in new positions. Note that the fingering doesn't change at all; the relationship among the notes remains the same on extended range basses, just as it does on four-string instruments.

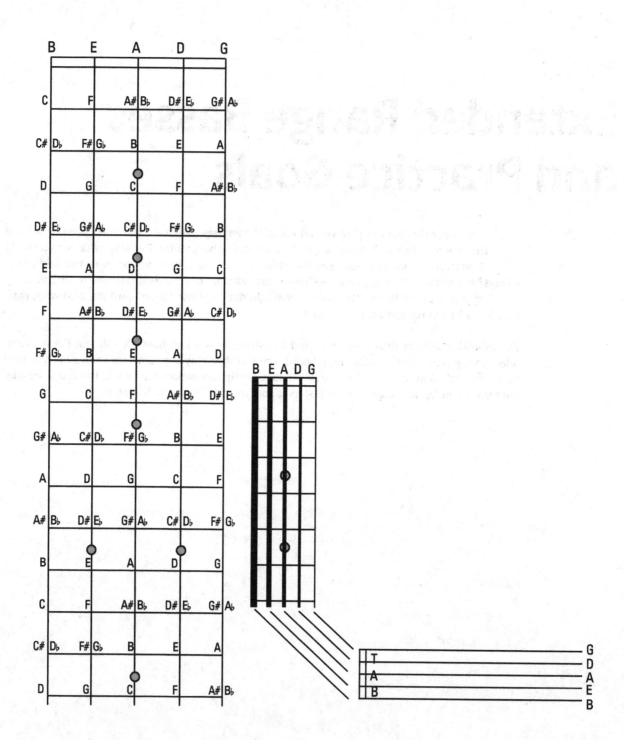

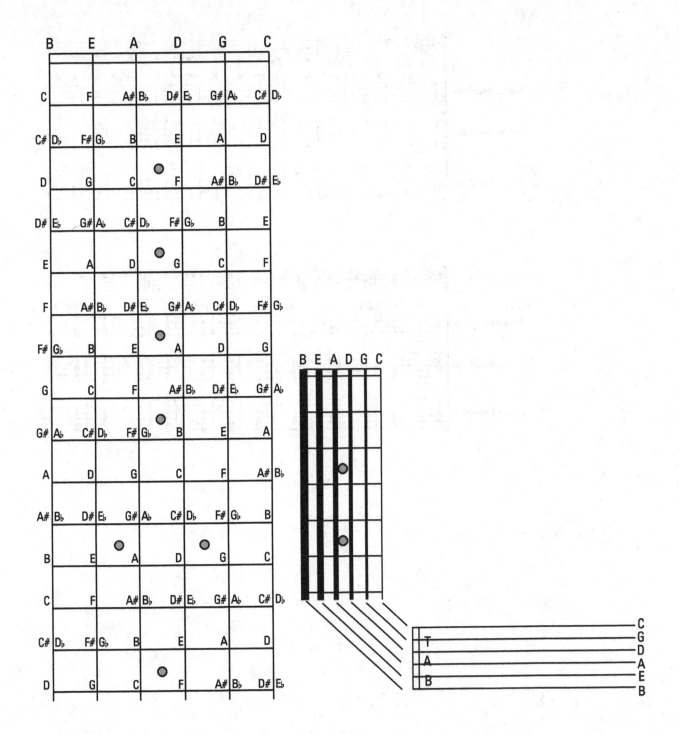

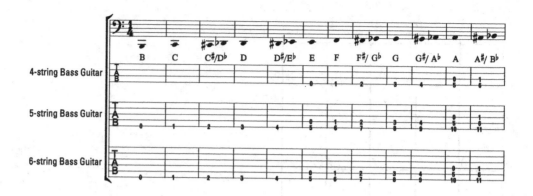

You can also find a weekly practice goal sheet at the end of this appendix, which I suggest you copy. Just fill in the exercises and songs you'd like to improve upon for the week, fill in the goal (for example: "Play exercise at 90 beats per minute," or "Know 'Donna Lee' by heart"), and then track your progress through the course of a week (seven days last I checked, despite the Beatles' claim of "Eight Days A Week"). By the end of the week you can see how close you came to achieving your objective. Then you can either repeat the exercise and up the ante or find a new goal to work on. Make sure you enjoy the journey — and don't be too hard on yourself.

TIP

If you run out of practice sheets or yours got worn out because you were so enthusiastically thumbing through these pages, you can always get more by visiting my Web site at www.sourkrautmusic.com to download the latest practice sheet.

	DAY 1	DAY 2	DAY 3	DAY 4	DAY 5	DAY 6	DAY 7	GOAL
TECHNIQUE								
THEORY								
PERFORMANCE								

About the Author

Patrick Pfeiffer is a professional bassist, composer, clinician, author, and bass teacher in New York City. He earned his bachelor's degree in music from Arizona State University and his master's degree in jazz studies from the New England Conservatory of Music, where he studied with famed bassist Miroslav Vitous. Pfeiffer's solo CD *Fruits and Nuts* (recorded with his group Phoenix) earned stellar reviews and a recommendation from *Bass Player* magazine. Besides performing and recording, Pfeiffer teaches bass guitar at the world-renowned Katie Agresta Studio in New York and gives clinics on rhythm-section playing for bassists and drummers throughout the United States. His former students include Adam Clayton of U2, Jean-Louis Locas of Cirque du Soleil, Mark Wike of the Bogmen, Alec Such of Bon Jovi, and Nick diPierro of Her & Kings County. Other former clients include Red Ant Records, Polygram, and Arista Records.

Pfeiffer has performed and/or recorded with George Clinton, Jimmy Norman, Phoebe Snow, Slam Stewart, Paul Griffin, Bernard Purdie, Babatunde Olatunji, Sheila Jordan, George Russell, Margaret Whiting, Joe Lovano, Carlos Alomar, Hernan Romero, the Marvelettes, the KMA Allstars, and the Gary Corwin Dream Band, to name a few.

Besides *Bass Guitar Exercises For Dummies*, Pfeiffer is the author of the international bestselling *Bass Guitar For Dummies* (1st and 2nd editions, published by Wiley), as well as *Improve Your Groove: The Ultimate Guide for Bass* (published by Hal Leonard) and *Daily Grooves for Bass* (published by Carl Fischer).

Pfeiffer is cofounder of Bass Remedies, Inc. (www.bassremedies.com), a company offering not only Internet-based video lessons but also live bass seminars featuring today's bass stars.

Dedication

This book is dedicated to the love of my life, my beautiful, lovely Lisa Ann Herth Pfeiffer.

I am buoyed by your love and balanced by your Reiki.

Author's Acknowledgments

My love and heartfelt gratitude to my wife and Reiki Master Lisa for her love, strength, wisdom, healing, and support whenever I find myself immersed in yet another big bass project. Your beautiful Reiki sessions are the reason I'm still standing tall after writing three books in two years. A huge thank-you to my wonderful friends: my tireless pre-editor Crissy Walford, a wonderful advocate for bass players and the English language; and Nick diPierro for the nightly bombing runs of special art. It is my supreme privilege to have two amazing musicians on the recording of this book's CD: Michael D'Agostino on drums and Sean Harkness on guitar. An additional thank-you to Michael D'Agostino for also expertly recording and mixing the CD in his professional studio. Special thanks to Shawn Setaro for proof-playing my exercises. I am very grateful for the love, encouragement, and support I've always gotten from my parents, Ursula and Wilhelm Pfeiffer. Parents everywhere should help their kids follow their dream, even if it means having a musician in the family. Mine did.

My utmost respect and thanks to the amazing *For Dummies* crew: Tracy Boggier, Natalie Harris, Alicia South, Todd Lothery, and all the people behind the scenes whom I never got to meet but who gave vital contributions toward the creation of this book. You all are a powerful team, and I am grateful for the long hours you've put in to make sure this book is the best it can possibly be. It has been a privilege and a pleasure to work with you. I hope you can implement some of my new terminology for future music books (such as BEOMD: By End Of *Musician's* Day . . . anytime before sunrise the next day). A special thanks to Marla Marquit Steuer for pointing the right folks in the right (my) direction, and a big thank-you to my incredible agent Bill Gladstone. I am indeed privileged to be associated with you. Thanks to all the people at Waterside Productions. I'd also like to thank the great Will Lee: You have been instrumental in my career and a wonderful inspiration. To my students, past, present, and future: I'm grateful for every lesson you teach me and every lesson you take from me. A special thanks goes to my brothers Andreas and Mark for their encouragement and support. I'm proud of you.

I'm very grateful to my teachers: Hilmar Stanger, Bruce Amman, Robert Miller, Dennis Sexton, Frank Smith, Chuck Marohnic, Jeff Andrews, and Miroslav Vitous. I carry your lessons with me. A special thanks goes to Reiner Hoffmann — you gave me my start in the bass world by gifting me your bass; to Michael Tobias for building my precious MTD basses; and to Jason DeSalvo, Joey Lauricella, and Vinny Fodera of Fodera basses. I'm very grateful to Michael Carolan for giving my music a chance to be heard by the world, Lawrence Green for getting me started in New York, and Katie Agresta for so many things. You are incredible friends whom I'll never forget. Thank you, Adam Clayton — you never cease to amaze and inspire me. Thanks to Julie Hanlon, Dee Behrman (my coach), Loys Green, Mike Visceglia, and Ronal Sanchez.

I am grateful to the beautiful people who are no longer with me but whose love and support have left an indelible imprint on my life: Marjorie Herth, Sandy Green, Paul Griffin, Gary Corwin, Mike Kissel, Bill Evans (the bass player), and Lance Berry.

And a very special thanks to LuLu for being a source of unconditional love and to Juba Muktananda (may I one day be as good a person as you think I am already).

A special thanks to Gurumayi Chidvilasananda of the Sidha Yoga Foundation and to Daisaku Ikeda and the SGI family.

Publisher's Acknowledgments

Project Editor: Natalie Faye Harris

Acquisitions Editor: Tracy Boggier

Copy Editor: Todd Lothery

Cover Photo: © jjwithers/Getty Images

Production Editor: Tamilmani Varadharaj